PENGUIN BOOKS

WRIT AT LARGE

Fahri Azzat is the managing partner of Messrs Fahri, Azzat & Co., a commissioner for oaths, a notary public, and a member of the Malaysian Bar Council. He studied law at Bristol University, United Kingdom, and graduated in 1997. He was admitted to the Malaysian Bar on 6 August 1999 and has been in practice since.

He authored the *Malaysian Guide to Advocacy* (2019, Sweet & Maxwell). He regularly contributes to authoritative practitioner's texts such as the *Malaysian Civil Procedure* and *Bullen & Leake & Jacob's Malaysian Precedent and Pleadings.*

He was also a founding member of LoyarBurok, a groundbreaking Malaysian legal blog, in 2006. He now writes regularly every Friday on his blog, *From the Bar Stool*, which he started on 8 October 2020.

Fahri Azzat lives and works in Selangor, Malaysia, with his parents, wife, four children, and four cats.

ADVANCE PRAISE FOR *WRIT AT LARGE*

'Books written by lawyers are often either turgidly technical or self-obsessively grandiose. Fahri Azzat's book is, on the other hand, nothing like that. He is opinionated (frequently!) and exasperating (at times) in his life and law views, but I love that about his book. I don't see it as one written purely for his fans who, though I am sure, must number many. This book calls for a response from the reader. If you want to be provoked, challenged, and teased, do leaf through this "dip and digest" book. You will not be disappointed.'

—Dr Jason Chuah, dean of the Faculty of Law,
University Malaya

'In *Writ at Large: A Legal Life Well-Rounded*, Fahri has written delightfully and insightfully about the sentiments, experiences, and insights of a senior and mature lawyer with a broad practice. With each story, he thoughtfully articulates the Malaysian experience while sharing with us the highs and lows of legal practice. I highly recommend this read. It will leave you enlightened, entertained, edified, and maybe even inspire you to take up law.'

—M. Kula Segaran, deputy minister, Prime Minister's
Department (Law and Institutional Reform)

'Few lawyers can tell stories about legal practice compellingly. Rarer is the lawyer who makes us feel as if we are right beside them conducting their case. With this collection, [Fahri] achieves both. His criminal cases read like thrillers. His meditations and stories about general legal practice are as entertaining as illuminating. If you are looking for a slice of legal life, the Malaysian experience, and a good read, this is the one.

—Edmund Bon Tai Soon, advocate and solicitor,
representative of Malaysia to the
ASEAN Intergovernmental
Commission on Human Rights

Writ at Large

A Legal Life Well-Rounded

Fahri Azzat

PENGUIN BOOKS
An imprint of Penguin Random House

PENGUIN BOOKS

Penguin Books is an imprint of the Penguin Random House group of companies whose addresses can be found at global.penguinrandomhouse.com

Published by Penguin Random House SEA Pte Ltd
40 Penjuru Lane, #03-12, Block 2
Singapore 609216

Penguin Random House SEA

First published in Penguin Books by Penguin Random House SEA 2025

10 9 8 7 6 5 4 3 2 1

ISBN 9789815233827

Typeset in Garamond by MAP Systems, Bangalore, India

www.penguin.sg

This book is dedicated to my beloved children, Seth Azzat, Ari Azzat, Qaim Azzat, and Fia Azzat.

May all of you live a life of meaning, beauty, and joy.

Contents

A GENERALLY CIVIL PRACTICE

GROWING UP AND ABOUT LEGALLY

Preface

I am delighted and proud to present this collection of essays from my blog, *From the Bar Stool.* All of them were revised, some lightly, some heavily, to reflect the change of circumstances since they were first written, as well as corrections and editorial revisions. The substance of the pieces, however, remains untouched. This published version stands as the authoritative version of these essays.

One of my goals with *Writ at Large* is to articulate the experience of Malaysian legal practice through the lens of a critical-minded, earnest legal practitioner who graduated from England but completed his Certificate of Legal Practice at the University of Malaya, before they closed that programme down, and practised in his father's firm for sixteen years and five months before establishing his firm in 2016, where he has been practising since.

Why? Two reasons.

Firstly, I felt there was, and remains, a dearth of literature available about lawyers, legal practices, and legal experiences that are not often, if ever, the subject of consideration or discussion in Malaysia. I wanted to raise and consider for discussion all things and aspects of legal practice, from the petty to the profound and everything in between, supported by good writing—something akin to Rousseau's *Confessions* but not *that* personal.

Secondly, I enjoy writing. I want it to be a compelling factor for reading, in addition to the subject matter of a piece. With my writing, I want to convey what it was like when I underwent those experiences, as vividly as possible. When I narrate my legal experiences I want you, the reader, to feel as if you were next to me—strapped in, eyes wide shut. I want you to feel my lesson learned emphatically, so hopefully, you know how to avoid it.

The main theme of this collection is to give the reader a sense of the goal I mentioned earlier, but in an abridged version.

The first eighteen chapters are mostly stories from my criminal legal practice or relate to them, except chapter twelve, which is about a civil legal aid case. I start with these because they are comparatively more exciting in terms of drama.

In chapter nineteen, I speak up for the generalist position in legal practice. We are commonly advised to specialize. I disagree.

In chapters twenty to thirty-two, I share my experiences as a pupil master, mentor, employer, and senior lawyer related to administrating a firm, dealing with seniors and the junior experience.

In chapter thirty-three, I share an anxiety from my early legal years. It is sometimes hard to see the future when one is stuck doing routine low-level work for several years.

In chapters thirty-four to thirty-seven, I discuss the other dimensions of my legal practice—conveyancing and corporate transactions, Syariah practice, and my work as an oaths and affirmations officer. These are less discussed and documented experiences.

In chapter thirty-eight, I mock those who describe themselves as 'non-practising advocate and solicitor'.

In chapter thirty-nine, I discuss the anxieties and pitfalls that arise from a profession that constantly demands us to be right, accurate and correct.

Finally, in chapter forty, I consider the elevated status of a lawyer in Malaysia in the context of retired judges practising as lawyers and appearing in court to argue.

Each chapter is episodic. You need not read the stories and essays in sequence except for the 'Hasan Ali and Me' series. Each can be read independently of each other. However, reading them sequentially will allow you to better appreciate certain ideas and concepts.

I would be delighted if you found this carefully selected collection pleasing, entertaining, and insightful, either in whole or in part. I can be reached at fahri@fromthebarstool.life.

—Fahri Azzat
March 2024

A TIME FOR CRIME

Not Risking Death

I have acted for several Africans who arrived on our Malaysian shores. All of them were charged with drug trafficking under section 39B of the Dangerous Drugs Act 1952 ('DDA52')[1], an offence punishable by death.

A majority of them were caught at the airport entering Malaysia. They often carried luggage that contained, among other things, items in which drugs were hidden inside. I call such cases 'fish-in-the-barrel' cases.

The facts fall within a very narrow compass. There is little time, too few characters, and the slimmest sliver of opportunity available for reasonable doubt to emerge. Their defences are usually disbelieved and dismissed.

The most common narrative of 'airport cases' is that the accused came to Malaysia for business or study. They were asked by a 'Chief', their boss or uncle, as a favour to carry some items (like soap, shoes, powder tins, a small bag) over to give to their employee, nephew, or friend here. Inevitably, the accused is caught upon arrival. The recipient, however, is uncontactable. Chief is unreachable. The police will not fly

[1] Act 234 Dangerous Drugs Act 1952 (Revised 1980) (1980) Pharmaceutical Services Programme. Available at: https://pharmacy.moh.gov.my/sites/default/files/document-upload/dangerous-drugs-act-1952.pdf (Accessed: 16 December 2024).

to the relevant African country to investigate and verify the accused's story.

The details may vary, but this is the DNA of fish-in-the-barrel cases. Since no one supports the accused's narrative, his explanation is inevitably considered a bare denial or an afterthought.

It is pretty much a sure-lose case. The reported cases are replete with examples.

Then, there are the 'fish-in-the-pond' cases.

The usual setting is where the accused is arrested in an open space, a house, or an apartment. In such situations, the accused is not tightly boxed in time and space and in the company of more people. An example of such a case is when an accused is caught in a police raid. Many officers are assigned to a drug raid; anywhere between five to fifteen officers are involved. The more officers there are, the more versions are likely to arise and potentially contradict each other. It's the Rashomon effect. A variety of versions provides space for reasonable doubt to emerge.

A fish-in-the-pond case was the one my Nigerian client named Obu faced. He was charged with trafficking dangerous drugs for a bag of drugs found in an apartment that had three other Nigerians with him at the time of arrest. Sixteen officers, bearing heavy firearms, raided the apartment. For some reason, the other three Nigerians were not charged. Obu was left to defend the charge alone.

The thing about Obu was he was unlike any of my previous African drug offence-related clientele until that point and even today. This is because he was highly educated, which was unusual for my usual run of clients charged with drug trafficking. My other African clients generally were less educated and often did not go on to secondary school if they managed to finish primary school. Their English was rudimentary. Many were poor and inarticulate. They were simple folk sent on a fool's errand caught in a hangman's noose because their lives are considered cheap and the law unforgiving. Desperation exuded from their pores.

Obu was different. He was intelligent, articulate, and cultured. He was an economics graduate.

His story went like this: An employment agency in Lagos told him they had secured him a job in Malaysia as a finance executive in a company. Obu paid the fees to his agents, who arranged for his visa and flight. When he arrived in Malaysia, he met with an agent who took his passport on the pretext of sorting out his work permit. He booked a hotel room so he could rest and be ready for his job. When Monday came, there was no company or job. He called the agent, who did not respond and could not be found.

Obu was screwed. He had only enough money for a week at the place he was staying. After that was over, he had none.

He went looking for work but wasn't taken seriously because he didn't have his passport. It also did not help that he was Nigerian. He said he could not even get to the point of showing prospective employers his credentials. Most of the time, they refused to let him in. He said that after staying in Malaysia, he realized he should not have come because we did not like his kind.

He resolved to find legitimate work to save enough money to buy a flight ticket home. Although Obu knew of other Nigerians in Malaysia, he understood what his countrymen were infamous for within his first week, so he stayed away from them. He said he did not want to be associated with them or hang out with them, lest he get caught for something they did. But that also meant he could not get into the expatriate Nigerian circles in Malaysia either.

Since Obu could not get a job, he decided to trade. At an exorbitant rate of interest, he borrowed money from a moneylender to buy items to sell, such as pens, belts, lighters, etc., at *mamak* shops, eateries, and open stall areas. Sales were tough.

'If I sold fifty ringgits worth in a week, it's like Christmas,' he told me.

He slept wherever he could: in alleys, under bridges, and anywhere he found shelter and security, no matter how fleeting. He showered in public toilets and used those in malls. Obu did that for almost a year, then gave up. All he managed to do that year was pay back the interest on the borrowed sum.

Since doing things the legitimate way did not get him anywhere, Obu decided to bite the bullet and look for fast but risky money. He would do what he could to get the money as quickly as possible in order to get his passport reissued, buy his flight ticket, and get out of Malaysia.

He fell in with a Nigerian group who were looking for fellow countrymen to help with their drug-selling operation. He was on probation with them for a week, following whoever he was assigned to learn the ropes. But as luck would have it, Obu was arrested in the apartment with his cohorts at the end of his first week.

I was the court-assigned counsel for Obu's case.

When I first spoke to him in prison, I sensed a difference about him. He understood his predicament and chances. When we discussed his case, it was as if we were discussing someone else's civil claim.

He was calm, collected, and rational.

We spoke often during the trial breaks, and I looked forward to it.

It started when I asked him, 'Do you know who Chinua Achebe is?'

When he replied, 'Of course!' I knew we were going to hit it off.

We did. From African literature to English literature to life in Lagos, common national issues, racial issues, social issues, and the like—he was well-informed, well-read, and possessed a cosmopolitan outlook. Obu was also a natural conversationalist.

Or maybe it was all a lie. Perhaps he was a master storyteller. But Obu felt and talked pretty real.

I ended up believing and liking Obu, feeling an intellectual kinship with him. I even caught myself wishing the trial would drag out a little more so we could have more breaks where I could enjoy conversations with him. But I also wondered what I would do in his situation: in a foreign country, where I stood out like a throbbing sore thumb, with the society prejudiced against me? Would I have done it differently? Could I have done so? Would I eventually succumb to illegal means in such a desperate situation? Was that justified?

Before the trial, I wrote in for a plea bargain, but that was rejected. So, the trial commenced and chugged along. The defence had little interest until it came to the raiding officers' testimony. After cross-examination, they gave such varying accounts of the events, along with insensible explanations, that there was serious doubt about who had been where, when, what had happened, and how.

Even though things looked better for Obu, we still were not done with the rest of the prosecution evidence. I did not think that was decisive enough for the defence to succeed, although the situation had the potential for it. The investigating officer had not yet been called. He could potentially repair vital shortcomings in the prosecution's case to a ready audience.

So, the case was too soon to call; in fact, it is always too soon to call a case.

After the last raiding officer left the witness stand during the trial break, the Deputy Public Prosecutor approached me and said he was interested in the plea bargain we had written earlier. I said I would take it to Obu, to whom I explained how the case was finely balanced at the moment. I even felt there might be a shot at winning, but I did not know how much. If he lost, the cost of that shot was the prospect of death. Or he could plead guilty to a lower possession charge but with an enhanced sentence. A lower charge would lead to imprisonment for a minimum of five years to life, with a minimum of ten lashes of the whip.

'You decide for me, Sir. You know best,' he told me.

'I cannot decide for you, Obu. I can only advise you. You have to make the decision yourself.'

'I know,' he assured. 'But I know you and trust you to make the right decision.'

No amount of persuasion would make him relent, so I decided to think it over and then decide. The court adjourned the trial for three days so that we could consider the plea bargain.

What made me hesitate to accept the reduced charge offer was that we *might* get more favourable witnesses as we went along. There was the niggling, lingering sense of it. But to decide on a case of this magnitude based on a vague sense of feeling felt flimsy. The other thing that made me hesitate was that Obu would be whipped and imprisoned for a long time if he accepted the plea bargain, which didn't sit well with me. I thought he was an unlucky man who did not deserve his misfortune, a good but unfortunate man forced to bow to a system that despised and shunned him.

I strongly felt he deserved an acquittal from his situation, not just his charge.

It felt wrong that Obu's potential would be whipped, split, and destroyed over the next decade in prison. I turned the case over and over in my mind to find something else to give me some psychological assurance that we had a chance for an acquittal. There was none. It was what it was. Nothing could give me any assurance or comfort that it was better to fight it out. All this took place over three feverish, anxious, and sleepless nights until the day for continued trial. We would proceed with it if the plea bargain did not happen.

Despite the anxiety I was put through, I did not regret it because I felt it gave me moral clarity in deciding. Or so I thought.

When Obu was brought into court, I went to him and told him what I had decided.

'Obu, I have decided for you to plead guilty. Because it means life. If you ask me to choose between the certainty of life with imprisonment and the possibility of freedom with the risk of death, I will choose life. I don't know what life that is or will be, but it is life nonetheless. What do you think?'

'You don't think I can win?' he replied.

'I feel like maybe we could—but it's a big, big maybe. I am not willing to risk your life to find out.'

'Very well. Do you know how many years I will get?'

'I don't know. The DPP didn't want to agree. He preferred to leave it to the judge. So, we will have to argue about the sentence. But ten strokes are guaranteed because it's the minimum. Same with the five years in prison. The judges have no choice with that.' I explained.

'Alright then. I will plead guilty to the other provision.'

Obu accepted the plea bargain and pleaded guilty to the reduced charge. I laid out his circumstances as I described them earlier to the judge to argue for a minimum sentence. Despite a lively sentencing hearing, the judge decided on 'sentencing trends' and sentenced Obu to sixteen years and ten strokes.

After the judge adjourned and departed, Obu slid back the latch from the dock and lumbered out. He did not rush but seemed dazed as he unsteadily exited the dock. I was walking back from the interpreter's table to my side of the table, when Obu appeared in front of me and cried. His body shuddered with his sobs. His calm and collected front collapsed.

'Oh god. Oh my god. Oh my god,' he bellowed.

I didn't know whether to pat him on the back or run. Was he angry at me? The court officers were up and approaching us. Obu dropped to his knees and continued sobbing.

'Thank you, God. Thank you. Thank you, God. Oh, God!' he repeated through a grimace, his eyes firmly shut, the tears streaming out his eyes. Maybe not?

It felt as if he was conveying a mix of conflicting feelings simultaneously. It was heart-wrenching to watch.

The court officers rushed over to help Obu up. They cuffed him and led him out. As he walked out, he recovered his composure and called out to me.

'I am sorry about my reaction. I was upset at hearing the sentence. Thank you for your help, Sir. And for the conversations. It's been a while since I could have such chats with anyone here. Thank you. Goodbye.'

The court officers took him to the courtroom lock-up. I was sad to see him go. That was the last time I saw Obu.

I thought back to what I had said to him: certainty of life with imprisonment—wasn't that a kind of death? Also, freedom at the risk of death—wasn't that just life? So much for moral clarity. I don't know what I would have chosen for myself. It was death on one hand and a kind of death on the other. Neither bore any appeal.

I packed my things, returned to the office, and closed my file on Obu's case.

Right Up to the Hilt

Donatus Chidera Okonkwo was arrested at the airport and charged with drug trafficking.

I remember him because of his name, specifically, his last name—Okonkwo. It is the name of the protagonist of one of my favourite novels, *Things Fall Apart*, by the Nigerian writer Chinua Achebe. It was a pioneering novel that challenged English literature's colonialist outlook to Nigeria, for it told the Nigerian narrative from the native point of view, instead of the Western colonialists'. It is short enough to read in one sitting, which is how I recommend reading it, to feel the full emotional impact of its ending.

I was excited to meet Donatus when I saw his name on the Shah Alam High Court appointment letter. I imagined he would be impressed with my knowledge of his tribe and village in Nigeria. However, our meeting on the first case management date was rather anticlimactic. He was the usual court-assigned foreign drug trafficking client: poor, uneducated, and simple. He was solely interested in how he would get out of his situation.

His case was the 'fish-in-the-barrel' type, which meant there was only a sliver of narrative from which one could fashion a defence.

Donatus's story went like this: His boss, Chief, had asked him to fly to Malaysia to pass on some items to Chief's brother,

Izu, who was studying there. After landing, Donatus received a call from Izu to set up a meeting. Later, Izu called him again after clearing customs. Donatus mentioned saving Izu's number in his phone. Izu had told him to wait at the airport until a pick-up could be arranged. So, Donatus stayed at the airport overnight.

The next morning, Izu called Donatus to tell him he could leave the airport. After clearing immigration, Donatus picked up his bags and had them scanned. The officer at the X-ray machine detected contraband inside and arrested him. Donatus was led to an inspection room and searched. They opened his bag in front of him using the keys found on him. Among the clothes, they discovered a pink bag.

It contained several bars of soap, a few tins of powder, and pairs of slippers. The soap bars had been hollowed out. While the top part of the powder tins contained powder, the bottom part was empty. The soles of the slipper were thickened and hollowed out as well. All these items, the police found, contained drugs—mainly small, tightly wrapped, and bound plastic packets containing methamphetamines. The police officers discovered this after making a few deft incisions into some of the items.

Of course, Donatus claimed he knew nothing about the drugs. All he knew was that Chief had wanted him to deliver those items to Izu, which were in the pink bag. Donatus said he had checked the items to make sure they were legitimate, but his probe had been limited to a visual inspection of the items in the bag. He explained he did not physically inspect them because he did not want to offend Chief.

It was the usual drug mule story.

Usually, the defence lawyer lacks evidence to corroborate the accused's narrative, especially since the important part of the event takes place overseas. The Malaysian police will not fly to Africa to verify the accused's story because the courts don't require them to do so. It is economical and convenient for the police and courts to treat their stories as mere denial or an afterthought, instead of something to be given the benefit of the doubt and investigated.

The only thing Donatus had going for him was Izu's mobile number being saved in his phone. He was certain that Izu had called him when he was at the airport. I thought if we could present Izu's mobile number in his phone's call history then we would have a chance at creating doubt in the prosecution's case, making Donatus's narrative a bit more believable.

We needed something as evidence, because the courts rarely accept the innocent carrier defence of 'I didn't know I was carrying drugs.' This absence of knowledge has to be proven; it is impossible to succeed unless the carrier can prove they have Alzheimer's. Proving a negative is always a tall order.

Moreover, any failure to inquire on the carrier's part is categorized under the concept of 'wilful blindness'. The law expects the drug mule to conduct due diligence on the items they carry. But this is where the law fails to appreciate the practical realities and relationships that discourage a drug mule from inquiry. One side has power and money, while the other does not. In fact, the latter often lacks education and standing in society. The former can send any number of the latter as mules wherever they please because their lives are considered cheap. To expect the disadvantaged to hold the powerful accountable is laughable and shows the wilful ignorance of the law towards human affairs.

I asked Donatus how confident he was about having saved Izu's number on his mobile phone. He was very certain.

When I asked if he was lying to me, he denied. I pressed him again, asking if he was absolutely certain because this would be the defence we would go ahead with; he would live and die by this defence. He assured that he was very certain of Izu's number being there.

Satisfied with his insistence and confirmation, I ran Donatus's defence on the claim that he was an innocent carrier, that is, he did not know he was carrying drugs. If Izu's mobile number had been saved on his phone, we could check the call log from the call history and prove the same. Izu's existence, independently and objectively verified, would lend credence to Donatus's innocent carrier defence, which could raise reasonable doubt about the drug trafficking charges against him. At every trial date, I asked him to confirm Izu's number was saved on his phone.

The prosecution had Donatus's phone, and our strategy was to challenge their case as best as we could. We wanted to put forth our defence and prove Donatus innocent by switching on the phone and showing the court the call history. Voilà—a hot serving of reasonable doubt.

We hoped an acquittal would follow.

The defence was inevitably called, as it is for 'fish-in-the-barrel' cases.

On the morning of the trial, I sought permission to inspect and switch on Donatus's mobile phone before the proceedings began. To my disappointment, it was dead and wouldn't switch on. Upon inspection, the court interpreter pointed out that the battery was damaged. When the case was called up, I asked the Judge to delay it until the afternoon because I wanted to find a replacement battery for the mobile phone. The moment the Judge allowed the stand down, an intern, my colleague Asim Ng, and I rushed to what is now known as the SACC Mall in Shah Alam to find a new battery.

Our challenge was the mobile phone and time. It was an old Nokia phone, at least three generations old. Finding the battery for it would be difficult, and we only had one hour.

The three of us split up to explore various parts of the mall. After each of us interrogated every mobile phone vendor, we finally found a battery we could use at a modest shop tucked away from the main shopping corridors. Even though it wasn't an original, but a substitute, the saleslady assured us it would work. She said no one sold the original battery anymore. We took her word for it, paid, and left.

We grabbed a bite on the way out and headed back to court. I must admit that I was anxious: If the battery did not work, Donatus's defence was doomed. I was full of nerves as I slid the battery into the phone and pressed the power button. The phone's screen lit up and emanated a faint green glow. It worked! Our battery hunt was not for nought! I switched off the phone and sat at the Bar table, pleased with our efforts.

As I waited for the case to be called up, I imagined Donatus triumphantly showing the call history to the judge with Izu's name in it, his arm outstretched confidently holding the phone, and the DPP looking to the heavens in despair with their hands frozen in a half-grip. Perhaps after that, we could determine whether Izu's number was local or international. I even imagined calling Izu's number right then and there. Victory felt close. I couldn't wait for the case to be called up. I recall thinking that if we won, it would be my first 'airport case' win.

Finally, the case was called up. Donatus was sworn into the box. I began with the examination-in-chief. After having him narrate how Donatus ended up in Malaysia, we reached the point in the story when Izu called him.

'You said Izu called your mobile phone. Where is your mobile phone?' I asked.

Donatus pointed to a phone, which lay on the table nearby.

'It is a Nokia phone. I see it on the table there. How many times did Izu call you?'

'Three times,' replied Donatus.

'Please tell the court when Izu called you each time.'

'Izu call me first time when I was landing. I saw missed call from him. I call him back. I tell him I am going to take the luggage. After I take my luggage, he called me. He asked me wait at the airport until he call again. I waited a long time. I sleep at the airport. While I wait for him I save his number in my phone. In the morning, Izu call me to meet. Then I go to immigration.'

'Does your Nokia phone show who called you?'

'Yes.'

'Is this the phone you saved Izu's number on?'

'Yes.'

'So, if you turn on your phone, we will find Izu's name and number in it?'

'Yes.'

'My Lord, permission for the witness to turn on his mobile phone.'

'Granted,' said the Judge.

'Mr Donatus, please turn on your phone and show the court Izu's name and number.'

He turned on the phone. I was on my feet, staring intently at Donatus: All eyes were on him and the phone. It took a while to boot up, as old Nokia phones do. I saw Donatus press the power button, and the screen flickered to life. The court was silent; only the air conditioner hum filled the room.

Donatus took longer than he should have. I was impatient and couldn't wait for him to hold up the phone. But he kept pressing the phone buttons. My heart dropped with each passing second. I don't know for how long he did that, but after what felt like an eternity, Donatus finally turned to me.

'It is not here, Sir.'

This was not the answer I expected or appreciated. But given the time he took, I knew there was no other answer. At that moment, I finally gave in to the possibility that he had lied to me.

His defence was over.

'Well, Mr Donatus, where is it?'

'I think it is in my other SIM card. It is the SIM card from Africa.' This was another lie; until that moment, he had never brought up the existence of another SIM card.

'And where is that card?'

'I don't know.'

Nonetheless, I completed the rest of his examination. Later, I watched the DPP destroy his testimony in a cross-examination. After a short re-examination, I closed the defence's case. The Judge directed written submissions, fixed a decision date, and adjourned the day.

As Donatus was led from the witness box to the holding cells, he looked at me. He noticed my look of deep displeasure when I approached him.

'Did I say something wrong, Sir?' he asked

'Yes, you lied to me, Donatus. There never was an Izu.'

'Will I be guilty, Sir?' he asked without missing a beat.

'Yes, Donatus. You will be.'

'Can you please do my appeal?'

'No, Donatus. I would not be good for your appeal.'

'Why?'

'Because if I did so, the appeal judges only need to ask me about your failed defence, which was conducted by me. Your appeal would be over in a minute. Get another lawyer: Hopefully, they can see or do something I can't.'

Donatus was convicted at the end of the trial. His plea to the Court of Appeal was dismissed.

His appeal to the Federal Court, too, probably met the same fate.

This is an example of why clients, whether in criminal or civil cases, should never lie to their lawyers. It harms the client more than the lawyer. A lying client suffers the consequences of those lies, while a lawyer only has their disappointment to manage.

Hasan Ali and Me

Part One

Prelude

Many years ago, when I was a young lawyer handling criminal cases from the Bar Council Legal Aid Centre, Kuala Lumpur (or KL LAC), I encountered a case that deeply affected me. It was around my fifth year of practice, in 2004.

The case involved a twelve-year-old Malay boy. I may have forgotten his name, but not his circumstances. He had been arrested for stealing an expensive mobile phone from a foreigner at a café. The retail price of the special edition mobile phone was a few thousand ringgits. Although the owner did not see him steal the phone, he was caught before he could escape. When I first read the facts, I remember thinking: *What a ridiculous sum to pay for a mobile phone!* Today, such prices for phones are common.

Unlike thieves of greater ambition, this boy was caught and sentenced by the juvenile court to Henry Gurney School, a school for juveniles, until he turned eighteen. I was appointed to conduct his appeal in the High Court against the sentence. However, he didn't dispute his conviction; he was the 'honest' sort of criminal who committed the offence but, when caught, confessed immediately.

I thought the sentence was harsh, but I understood the rationale behind it. Firstly, he committed the offence while already serving a probation order for a first offence. Breaching a probation order inevitably results in jail time. Secondly, his second offence was the same as his first: theft. The court frowns upon serial offenders; you get a pass on your first offence, but it's your arse on the line for the next.

Up until then, I had heard about Henry Gurney Schools, but hadn't felt the need to delve further, as I didn't frequently handle juvenile criminal cases. It was only after this sentence that I started researching Henry Gurney Schools and other government detention facilities for juveniles. Let me say that after doing so, I was certain that my client should not be sent there, and I resolved to do my best to convince the High Court judge.

I sought out someone who could testify about the state of these schools and centres in court and suggest alternatives. A friend recommended a well-known educationist, who proved to be a friendly, willing, and helpful witness. I was pleased because I did not know how else to demonstrate the unsuitability of those schools for reformation. However, even though her evidence was valuable, her participation only solved half the problem.

The next challenge was deciding where he should be sent, which was the bigger problem. The educationist recommended a private facility for troubled children, but that was improbable because the government wasn't likely going to pay for it. Understandably, they preferred their own detention and reform facilities for juveniles. The only viable option was his parents. After calling them up and laying out the options, they said they were prepared to take him back and watch over him. I secured the attendance of my client's parents and the educationist for the hearing date, and headed in with crossed fingers.

On the day of sentence hearing, I started strongly with the educationist, who gave an excellent testimony for us. Her eloquence and knowledge helped field the questions well, making me hopeful about persuading the Judge to avoid sending the boy to Henry Gurney.

Next, it was the parents' turn. However, I was worried they would not persuade the Judge of their ability to supervise their son properly, for I didn't get to meet them before the hearing. We only had one phone conversation to persuade them to attend the hearing and take responsibility for their son and my client.

I sat at the Bar table, close to the dock, where my client sat just within an arm's length from me. His parents appeared before the judge and stood side by side. Even though their backs were turned towards us, they were close enough for my client and me to hear their exchange with the Judge.

'What do you do, Sir?' asked the Judge.

'I am a small trader in Kuala Lumpur,' replied his father.

'And you, Madam?'

'I am a housewife.'

'Do you know why you are here today?'

They both nodded.

'Your son has committed theft again. He has breached his probation order. This is the second time he has stolen something. His lawyer is asking me not to send him to Henry Gurney School and instead consider releasing him back to your custody. He says you are committed to take responsibility for him this time. I summoned both of you here today because I want to hear directly from you whether you are capable of doing this. Wanting to take care of him is one thing, but whether you have the ability to do it is another matter altogether. So, I want to hear from each of you individually. Whoever is ready may speak first.'

After a moment's pause, the mother began.

'Yang Arif,[2] I hope you don't think poorly of me, but after thinking further about it, I am okay with sending him to Henry Gurney. I cannot take care of him, for he doesn't listen to me. When I scold him, he runs out of the house or talks back to me. I don't know where he goes; he doesn't tell me and comes back whenever he wants. I warned him to be careful after the first offence and to stay away from his friends, who got him into trouble the very first time. Yang Arif, I am sad about this, but maybe this is his fate. Yang Arif, he is my eleventh child out of twelve. There are too many of them. I cannot manage them. Maybe this is best for him.'

My heart sank upon hearing that. I saw my efforts go down the drain. I wondered how my client felt, having heard his mom speak of him like that in court before a Judge. I turned to look at him, but he seemed to be staring into some space of his own.

'So, what do you do during the day?'

'I do part-time work here and there because my husband's income is not enough, Yang Arif. I do some sewing, babysitting, cooking, cleaning, whatever—so long as it pays. I work every day and, on an average, I earn about 300–400 per month.'

'How much does your husband earn?'

'Between 1,500–2,000 per month. The rent takes up most of it. The rest goes for food and utilities. My income goes towards food only.'

'Anything else you want to say?'

---

[2] 'Yang Arif' is the Malay equivalent of 'Your Lordship'.

'No.' she said. The Judge turned to the father, who took his cue.

'Yang Arif, I will take responsibility for him. I know we didn't do well the first time, and I am very sorry for that. My son can be wilful sometimes—perhaps he is not suited for school education. If Yang Arif, gives me responsibility, I will take him with me to help me trade. Maybe that is what I should have done the first time. I promise to make this work, Yang Arif. He is not a bad boy. Yes, his friends are not a good influence on him, I acknowledge that. But I will keep him away from them and close to me. I believe if he is away from them, he will turn a new leaf.'

'Is what your wife said about your finances true?' asked the Judge.

'Yes, Yang Arif.'

'What do you sell?'

'I sell shirts, shoes, bags at Chow Kit, Yang Arif. I have a stall.'

I prayed the Judge wouldn't ask what sort, as it would not help our case.

'Who else works with you?'

'No one else, Yang Arif. He can be my helper.'

'Anything else you want to say?'

'Please grant us this last chance, Yang Arif. I promise to do my best. Thank you, Yang Arif.'

The court discharged the parents and turned to me.

'Well, Counsel, I have heard the evidence. While I am inclined to agree with you that your client should not be sent to Henry Gurney, the question is, where do we send him?'

'I understand, My Lady. I confess, having heard his parents, I don't feel confident about them either.'

'Precisely. The mother agrees to send him away. I doubt the father can keep this young man in check. I have little doubt in his mother's complaints. That rules them out. You can also rule out private detention facilities. That brings us back to Henry Gurney. But you do not want that.'

'It does seem like that, My Lady.'

'Or how about this, Encik Fahri, I release him into your custody on a bond of good behaviour for two years? You take responsibility for him. How about that? I am serious; I am prepared to do that.'

I was stunned at the proposal and unsure of how serious she was. Quickly running it through my mind, I warmed up to the idea, but realized I wasn't in a position—financially and facilities-wise, at that moment—to offer the boy a place to stay, never mind taking care of his education, food, and everything else.

'As much as I would like to give it a shot, I am not ready for something like that right now, Yang Arif,' I said.

'Well, that settles it, then. You see how difficult it is to place him, Counsel? You tried your best, but I'm afraid the situation is against you. His error was committing the second offence and breaching the probation order. The law is clear on that. Having heard his mother, I am fortified the sentence is appropriate. I dismiss the appeal and confirm the juvenile court's sentence. I hope he turns over a new leaf during his time there. This court is adjourned.'

The hearing was heartbreaking. I thought about the psychological impact and the consequence on my client of hearing his mother's words in court.

I don't know if he pursued further appeals.

Like many of my legal aid clients, this boy, too, faded from my life once the case ended. I rarely come across these clients again.

From that day onward, I hatched a personal project: The Second Chance Initiative. It would set me up to react better to a situation like that in the future. Next time, if a judge gave me such an opportunity, and if I felt the person deserved it, I would take them on, armed with the means to do so. The idea was to provide these deserving people a meaningful second shot at life, to help them build the fishing rod of their life, instead of feeding them fish.

This project and my drive for its realization led me to Hasan Ali.

Hasan Ali and Me

Part Two

Lude

Hasan Ali was my friend's legal aid client, who was convicted after pleading guilty to an offence under Section 6(1) of The Corrosive and Explosive Substances and Offensive Weapons Act 1958 [3] ('the Act') in the Sessions Court in 2016. I reproduce that provision below, along with two others, for a better understanding of this offence. It should also be of general interest to Malaysians because it could apply to those who carry a pocket or Swiss-army knife or *parang* even when they do not intend to harm anyone.

> (1) Any person who in any public road or place carries or has in his possession or under his control any offensive weapon otherwise than with lawful authority or for a lawful purpose shall be guilty of an offence and on conviction be liable to imprisonment for a term of not less than five years and not more than ten years.

---

[3] Corrosive and Explosive Substances and Offensive Weapons Act 1958 (Revised 1988) (1988) Common Lii. Available at: http://www.commonlii.org/my/legis/consol_act/caesaowa19581988652/ (Accessed: 16 December 2024).

What is an offensive weapon? This is defined in Section 2 of the Act as follows: '"Offensive weapon" includes any instrument which if used as a weapon of offence is likely to cause hurt . . .'

If it reads as broad as it sounds, you are inferring it correctly. And yes, if I were to take a pen and stab someone with it, that pen could fall under the statutory definition of an 'offensive weapon'. This reading holds true, even if we read the provision restrictively because it is an offence that can be punished with imprisonment. An offensive weapon, as defined, could include anything that causes pain. It does not have to be a weapon by invention to meet the terms laid out in section 6(1) of the Act.

But what level of hurt are we talking about?

Section 319 of the Penal Code[4] defines 'hurt' as:

> 'Whoever causes bodily pain, disease, or infirmity to any person is said to cause hurt.'

So, if the object causes someone physical pain, it meets the legal definition of causing hurt. My example with the pen fulfils all these yardsticks. If I were to stab someone in the neck with my uncapped fountain pen (which has a very fine nib), it would cause them bodily pain. Pressing a sharp point of an object against flesh is very likely to cause hurt. Now, my fountain pen is a writing *'instrument which, if used as a weapon of offence, is likely to cause hurt'*. Substitute my pen with my guitar; now it is a musical instrument, *which, if used as a weapon of offence, is likely to cause hurt.* The possibilities are limitless.

---

[4] Act 574 - Laws of Malaysia (2023) Malaysian Anti-Corruption Commission. Available at: https://www.sprm.gov.my/admin/files/sprm/assets/pdf/penguatkuasaan/Akta_574_(31.5.2023)_BI.pdf (Accessed: 16 December 2024).

Now that we are acquainted with the potential absurdity of this offence, let us return to Hasan Ali's sentence by the Sessions Court. He pleaded guilty and was fined RM 5,000 or two months-long imprisonment, if he's unable to pay. Since the prosecution was dissatisfied with the sentence, it appealed to the High Court. Hasan Ali didn't find legal representation at the Sessions Court or the High Court.

At the High Court, the prosecution argued the court was not bound by the minimum imprisonment term of five years. The Judge queried the DPP about the effect of the 2014 amendment to section 6(1). This amendment increased the original sentence for the offence from 'not exceeding two years' of imprisonment to a minimum of five years and a maximum of ten years—a severe hike to the statutory sentence for a 'minor' offence.

This passage from the High Court judgment, *Public Prosecutor v Hasan Ali Abdul Razak* [2016] 9 CLJ 584, in paragraph 11, is interesting:

> The Learned Deputy Public Prosecutor handling this matter indicated that she wanted to do some research on the issue of whether the minimum 5 years imprisonment sentence is mandatory. When this Court resumed the hearing, the learned Deputy Public Prosecutor did not render much assistance to this Court, for example, to make comparison with some other laws, such as offence of rape in the Penal Code and offence under the Dangerous Drugs Act 1952 which also provide the words 'not less than' in the section of the law. Instead, the learned Deputy Public Prosecutor submitted that because of the word 'be liable' is used in the amendment, the sentence of not less than 5 years imprisonment is not mandatory.

I find it curious that despite chiding the DPP for not drawing comparisons with other provisions, the Judge adopted the prosecution's argument as mentioned above. His Lordship eventually decided it was 'still open for the court to impose an order for a bond of good behaviour or to impose any sentence based on the sentencing principles'.

Because the word 'liable' is used in the phrase 'shall be liable to' in Section 6(1), it means a court can decide an alternate, less strict punishment, instead of imposing the stated one. It would be different if the phrase read 'shall be punished with'. The use of the word 'shall' in contrast with 'liable' implies a court must apply the stated sentence and that it cannot impose an alternate lesser punishment. That was essentially the Judge's reasoning. With that, he allowed the appeal and imposed a one-year prison term in addition to the fine by the Sessions Court, even though Section 6(1) provided a minimum imprisonment period of five years.

Hasan Ali couldn't pay the fine, so he served two months in prison. However, as the High Court added another year to his sentence, he faced an additional year.

However, the prosecution was still dissatisfied, despite the addition of a year to the sentence. They appealed the decision to the Court of Appeal, feeling duty-bound to obtain a minimum sentence of five years, as stated in Section 6(1).

My friend took up the case through the National Legal Aid Foundation. However, he felt it best to have someone with more criminal experience than him lead it, considering the case was in the Court of Appeal. Although he was happy with the High Court's decision, he harboured concerns about its correctness. His instincts turned out right: after reading the record of appeal, I told him I felt both the Magistrates and High Court erred in their respective decisions.

I agreed with the High Court's interpretation that Section 6(1) of the Act did not exclude the court from passing a sentence for a good behaviour bond instead of imprisonment. A good behaviour bond is essentially a suspended sentence, during which the convict will not be sent to prison. Usually, it is granted for two years; if the convicted person stays out of trouble during that time—which is, they do not breach the peace—they will be freed. But a violation would enable the court to arrest and sentence them severely for the initial offence. The prosecution did not contest this aspect.

However, I disagreed with the High Court's claim that it had retained discretion to impose another prison sentence, notwithstanding the stated minimum term. If the court wanted to impose jail, it had no choice but to sentence the offender to a minimum of five years. It had no discretion to impose 'any sentence', such as a fine or a one-year jail term because Section 6(1) did not permit those; imprisonment was the only sentence that could be passed.

Additionally, the Judge's interpretation of Section 6(1) undermined Parliament's intention to increase the sentence for the offence (whether rightly or wrongly; I think, wrongly). What was the point of stipulating a minimum sentence, if the court wasn't bound by it? This was the troubling consequence of the Judge's interpretation.

Having said that, I'd like to believe I understand the sentiment driving the Judge's decision. I write this presumptuously, of course, but we are not happy with the minimum sentence stipulated for that offence; it is disproportionate to the 'harm' done and fetters the court's discretion to fashion an appropriate sentence. I'd also like to believe we both agree the previous sentence of a maximum of two years was more appropriate. A sentence of five to ten years, however, for simply possessing an offensive weapon in a public place without lawful reasons is outrageous. This is not an offence for doing something with an offensive weapon but simply bringing it around in public.

As I have explained, we are all potentially vulnerable to prosecution under this provision. I live in a constant fear, because I carry at least four fountain pens on an ordinary day!

To add salt to the wound, the punishment for voluntarily causing hurt, under Section 323 of the Penal Code, is a maximum of one-year prison term, a maximum fine of RM 2,000, or both. Our client would get a far lighter sentence if they punch someone instead of standing around a public place with a pocket knife tucked away deep in their special lining pocket, doing nothing.

For myself, both the Magistrates and the High Court were correct in their sentiments but made legal errors. I explained this to my friend and told him we wouldn't be defending the High Court's decision because their interpretation of the law was indefensible. My strategy was to acknowledge that the High Court's decision was incorrect and argue for a bond of good behaviour because I felt the facts allowed us a shot at it. He agreed and wished us luck for the hearing, which was scheduled for 7 April 2017.

As is usual with my appellate clients, the day of the hearing is usually the first time I meet them. The same was true for Hasan Ali. I saw him from afar while I was at the Bar table; he sat in the dock. My friend facilitated dialogue between us where required. I usually leave the interview of the appellate criminal clients to my colleagues, who bring along a pupil or intern who usually are keen on prison visits.

There is no need to interview the client for an appeal because the battle arena is the petition, record of appeal, and submissions. Rarely is a client's account about what happened at the trial relevant to an appeal. This is because the issue in an appeal differs from the one at trial. At the latter stage, it is: *Did they do it or not?* On the other hand, the primary issue on appeal is: *Did the trial judge undertake any misdirection of law or make a perverse factual finding in arriving at his decision?*

This is evident only from the record and legal precedents, not further testimony. The primary issue at trial is a secondary issue on appeal. Only when the trial judge is demonstrated to have committed a serious error of law or facts, does an appellate court descend to re-evaluate a trial court's decision. Anything less does not suffice. However, if no serious error by the judge can be shown, the appeal will likely be dismissed.

It is a ceaseless source of pleasure and amazement when something takes places precisely as planned, imagined, or hoped for. That was how the hearing unfolded in Hasan Ali's case. The facts he pleaded guilty to were as follows:

On the afternoon of 14 April 2016, the complainant called the police to inform them he had detained Hasan Ali. As per the complainant, he had identified Hasan Ali from CCTV footage as the person who had stolen his wife's slippers and tried to steal gold chains from a nearby temple the day before. The police visited the complainant, searching for Hasan Ali, when they found a 30 centimetre-long knife in the bag he was carrying. Hasan Ali explained that he had recently bagged a job as a security guard for a water tank in Pandamaran and that the knife was for his protection while at work. That was his first offence.

The Court of Appeal panel thankfully shared my sentiment (and what I imagined the High Court Judge had felt) about the unreasonable and harsh nature of the amended sentence. Given the circumstances, they refused to impose the minimum sentence. I recall an exchange between the panel and the DPP during which the chairing judge remarked,

'You want us to sentence him to five years simply fir possessing a knife? Five years for that alone is unreasonable. Very harsh. He hasn't done anything.'

The Court of Appeal granted the appeal, but substituted the sentence with a bond of good behaviour for two years with a sum of RM 2,000 in one surety, without needing security. This meant all the surety had to do was sign off the bond, and Hasan Ali would be freed. They did not have to deposit a sum of money for security.

I was pleased with the decision and began thinking about lunch.

After sorting out Hasan Ali's bond, my friend suggested we leave. He left me to discuss that with the interpreter. While waiting, I went up to Hasan Ali to congratulate and acquaint myself with him. He was a thirty-five-year-old Indian Muslim, educated up to secondary school, who did many odd jobs because he couldn't find any regular work. He appeared scrawny and unkempt, with a sullen and sickly look, and had scabs on his hands. Hasan Ali was not a talker and spoke only when spoken to.

The bond arrangement took a while because they couldn't reach Hasan Ali's mother or friends to stand as surety. As his mobile phone was not returned to him, he couldn't remember their phone numbers. His attempts to recall also proved futile. My friend failed to get more information from the legal aid centre and grew annoyed because if we couldn't resolve his surety by 1 p.m., the prison officers would take Hasan Ali back to Sungai Buloh, where he would be remanded until someone stood as surety. So, unless there was a surety, all our good work would have been for nought. We were running out of time.

We gathered around the court around noon, thinking of Hasan Ali's options, when the Second Chance Initiative floated into my mind. Truth be told, it had always been lurking in the back of my mind. But I had gotten so used to looking for an opportunity, I forgot to act on it. By the time of Hasan Ali's case, it had been about ten or eleven years since the earlier incident. I had established my firm, acquired an apartment near the office, saved a small sum for being deployed, and had been seeking someone I felt deserved that second chance. This time, if the chance came, I was ready.

When the hour drew close to 1 p.m., I thought, perhaps, this was the person for my Second Chance Initiative. I sought the registrar's permission to interview Hasan Ali and consider stepping in as his surety. It was allowed. The court's police officer, a grandfatherly Malay chap with a contented look, escorted us into the holding cells in the basement of the Palace of Justice. It was my first time down there: This was a day of many firsts.

My chat this time with Hasan Ali was quick because the transport to Sungai Buloh was about to depart. He had no work and was unhappy staying with his mother due to his stepfather. Even though he wasn't a part of any gang, no one would hire him because he had no qualifications. After months of looking for steady work, guarding the water tank was his first decent job. He pleaded guilty because the knife was his, and he kept it for protection. This was his first conviction.

My terms were laid out: He would work for me as a dispatcher or driver for two years at a minimum wage and stay in accommodation I provided. He could get in touch with his friends or acquaintances but only with my permission—I wanted to gauge whom he hung around with. He would also need to take up a course—vocational or otherwise—to acquire a skill.

He agreed to all my terms, and we shook hands on it. His palm was coarse and scabbed in parts. A smile broke on his face; he thanked me with glassy eyes. The police officer who was with us urged Hasan Ali to be grateful for his good fortune and said that he had never heard of a lawyer stand surety for a convict before. It felt good to hear that.

It was like suddenly feeling the presence of an object in a pitch dark room where I'd been lost. It was disorienting, but there was progress despite the darkness. It also happened that the apartment I had acquired for the initiative was available then, which fortified my thought that perhaps I was on the right track. It was like finding another object in that pitch dark room, and had a sense of what I like to call 'a planet-aligned moment'. Things lined up as I had hoped, though I am powerless to affect anything in that order. I didn't align the planets; I merely had the privilege of being a witness.

By the time we settled the bond, it was well past lunchtime. I wanted to skip it to get Hasan Ali medically examined, as he had scratched his head and body and hands too often. He followed me back to the office, where I introduced him to my retinue of initially stunned lawyers (I had no staffers back then), who welcomed him warmly. After the introductions, I had my pupil take him to the clinic. The itching was due to scabies he had picked up in prison, and he was given medication to treat it. By night-time, we managed to collect enough basics for him to settle in the main room of the apartment, which was a five-minute walk from our office.

The next day, we met him again to buy the rest of the things for his comfort in the apartment. I told him to settle down and rest up on Sunday. He was to report for work the next day. Finally, after more than a decade, my Second Chance Initiative was up and running.

Hasan Ali and Me

Part Three

Between 2012 and 2016, just before I took Hasan Ali on, I had the good fortune to meet a few excellent people and establish satisfying relationships—both professional and personal—with them, which would prove to be inspiring. I hoped Hasan Ali would continue being a part of that good fortune run.

Through April and May of 2017, my lawyers and I took efforts to make Hasan Ali feel welcomed. He, however, kept to himself, speaking only when spoken to. When he wasn't working, he would sit in our library and watch videos on his phone. Nevertheless, he was obliging, always ready to attend to whatever was asked of him without complaint.

To make more opportunities for socializing with him, we became more diligent about planning firm lunches and dinners. My co-workers, Asim Ng and Rafeeza Hamdan, who exercised in the evening, invited him on their runs. Asim lifted weights at the time, so he had more opportunities to converse with Hasan Ali. My other colleagues, Farhan Haziq and Ameerul Aizat, worked closely with him because they managed the daily dispatches.

All four of my lawyers were gems: They contributed and took charge of their own accord without my word.

It was a spontaneous order: Everyone knew what to do, without coordination.

Hasan Ali was not a talker. Every time I tried to get a conversation going with him—after work, at a *makan*[5], or if I saw him around the office—it didn't get far. Sometimes we talked, most times we didn't. Occasionally, we just smoked wordlessly together, staring at our smoke tendrils blending before us in a swirling grey haze. He would answer all my questions, but our 'conversations' often found me examining him closely. Perhaps, he was not comfortable talking to me.

Hasan Ali was one of the many who ended up availing legal aid for criminal cases. He was one of the those who slipped unnoticed through the cracks of the educational and social support system, briefly surfaced like a whale leaping out of the ocean, that too only for his conviction and sentencing, before disappearing into social oblivion.

He never finished secondary school, worked a string of small jobs, and struggled to hold on to anything for more than two years at a time. His father had passed away some time ago, and his mother had, since then, remarried. His stepfather had a much younger son whom Hasan Ali got along with. However, his stepfather picked on him and treated him like an outsider. His mother didn't defend him when he was being dressed down, but tried to make it up later.

Hasan Ali was unhappy about the situation but didn't have enough money or stability to move out, especially since he gave his earnings to his mother.

After his first week with us, I suggested Hasan Ali visit his mother, who lived in Klang. We wanted her to know he

[5] A direct translation of 'makan' is 'eat' in Malay. Colloquially it is used as 'meal'.

was fine and had started his life anew in Pealing Jaya. When he returned, he reported she was pleased to know he was doing well.

Hasan Ali's time in prison had been awful. It was cramped, as he shared the cell with at least seven other inmates. As the new guy, he slept on the floor closest to the communal toilet, which was open and perpetually damp. He recounted its smell: It was something else, unforgettable, and sometimes, he could not help but remember it. There was also no mattress, so he slept on the filthy floor.

Everything had been a fight to keep. His rations and meagre possessions would be taken if he could not defend himself in jail. In his free time, he watched television with others, which only showed religious educational programmes. The food was bare sustenance—fish, rice, vegetables, and soup of poor quality. After a while, he gave up eating rice, and recalled its hard and inedible nature. Even though he knew his other fellow prisoners, he made no friends and kept to himself.

I digress for a moment to ponder briefly on the unfairness of our prisoners having to suffer above and beyond imprisonment and a regimented lifestyle. After the Covid pandemic, we can now comprehend the psychological impact of such confinement in our own homes. Despite decent food, internet access, social media, streaming services, and video conferencing at our disposal, there is a tugging, stifling sense of confinement and a natural desire to go out.

This underlines the importance of the freedom of movement, a fundamental liberty enshrined in Article 9(2) of the Federal Constitution.[6] It guarantees every Malaysian citizen

---

[6] Federal Constitution (2020) Malaysia Federal Legislation. Available at: https://lom.agc.gov.my/federal-constitution.php (Accessed: 16 December 2024).

the right to move freely throughout and reside anywhere in Malaysia, recognizing our human need to move about as we please, without restraint. However, this liberty isn't absolute and, thus, subject to any law relating to national security, public order, public health, or the punishment of offenders—meaning our liberty of movement can be curtailed, but only under serious circumstances.

How much worse will that sense of confinement be while living in a cramped prison room without access to our customary luxuries, with bad food, worse company, and filthy floors? Section 6(1) of The Corrosive and Explosive Substances and Offensive Weapons Act 1958 prescribes a minimum prison term of five years and a maximum of ten years. However, it doesn't prescribe that a convict should be treated poorly during imprisonment, as incarceration and a regimented lifestyle are the intended punishments and the extent of the legal sentence.

Poor treatment shouldn't form a part of a prisoner's legal punishment. It could be argued that poor food, living conditions, personal security conditions, etc., go far beyond the prescribed punishment or harm that can be lawfully inflicted. Hasan Ali picked up scabies during his imprisonment, which caused him immense discomfort.

Scabies is not an infection but an infestation. Tiny mites called *sarcoptes scabiei* set up shop on the outer layers of human skin, which doesn't react kindly to the invasion. The infestation leads to relentless itching and an angry rash as the mites burrow and lay eggs inside the skin. Is it fair or reasonable that he should be vulnerable and suffer that (and God knows what else) in addition to his incarceration?

In his early days with us, I tried him out as a driver, but he wasn't one. He was suited for the motorcycle. In his first month, Hasan Ali did well: He enjoyed being back on a motorcycle and even said happier to run the dispatches, which gave him an excuse to ride around. He was also early to work. By the second month, he didn't look so dour, though, he even smiled occasionally.

He seemed religious. He mentioned spending most of his free time at the *surau* near our office, finding peace there. I was happy to hear that and hoped the religious influence would prove to be an additional buffer to keep him on the right path. What I felt he needed were stable anchors and boundaries, which religion would offer if genuinely practised.

In June 2017, I rented out the other two rooms of the apartment Hasan Ali lived to three young Bangladeshi Muslim men. The leader of the three was Rahman, who spoke the best English, displayed intelligence, and had a pleasant demeanour. The other two merely smiled, nodded, and followed his lead. The men, with legitimate working permits, seemed nice and friendly enough, and worked at various shops near the Tesco supermarket. I was pleased because I didn't want Hasan Ali to be lonely in the apartment and hoped they would get along.

Although, what seemed like a good move at the time, became a decision I deeply regretted.

From June onwards, we grew busier with deadlines and hearings. Hasan Ali appeared to have settled into a routine at the firm. Each morning, he would arrive to collect the day's work and then return once done. When requested, he would show his logbook to the lawyers who assigned him work. We shared a smoke once in a while, during which I would ask him about his work and its progress. However, these grew shorter and less frequent as the work grew more intense.

Out of respect for his privacy, I largely left Hasan Ali to himself when he wasn't working or socializing with us. Although, I would check in with him randomly to enquire about his whereabouts and companions. His leisure time and weekends were his, and I didn't intrude into his personal space or time. I wanted him to have a life outside work.

Maybe, he felt it was unnecessary to invite me into his personal life. I recall a curious remark he made to me once, when I stated we had a nice, long upcoming weekend. He expressed a wish for no holidays so he could work all the time and said he didn't enjoy the weekends.

One day, in mid to late July, in the evening after work, Asim came to see me, suspecting Hasan Ali was drinking. I remember thinking, *Wait, that didn't jive with his hanging around the surau.* When I asked him what made him think so, he mentioned smelling alcohol off Hasan Ali on a few occasions.

If Asim smelled it on him, it must have been before or during office hours. While I hadn't noticed it myself, I assured him of future vigilance and asked Asim to report any suspicious behaviour from Hasan Ali to the rest of us.

Looking back, I should have investigated his suspicion immediately. Asim is sharp about people, and he calls it right, by my count, on most of our cases together. Instead, I got back to work, as we all were buried in our respective cases. Soon, it was forgotten. July and August were a blur.

Then, at approximately 11 a.m. on 30 August 2017, all hell broke loose.

The doorbell buzzed insistently. We heard footsteps scuffling up the stairs as soon as the front door was unlatched. It was the three Bangladeshis I had rented the rooms to. They arrived panting, dishevelled, and distressed, with tears streaming down their faces. I was completely shocked to see them like that.

'Rahman, what happened?' I asked.

It all came out in a torrent between taming his sobs and gasping for air:

'Sir, Hasan is crazy! He locked us in the apartment, took away our keys, and didn't let us out for the last few days. We could not go to work. He even took away all our money. When we couldn't give him any more money, he kicked and punched us.'

I was nonplussed and stood dazed for a moment.

'Sir, he's always drinking and consistently drunk. Every day, he's at it! When he is drunk, he becomes erratic and violent. We barely managed to escape, Sir. The moment he let us out, we ran straight to your office. He threatened to kill us, if we escaped.'

What the hell just happened? Once I faded back into autonomy, I felt my heart beating fast.

'Please, help us, Sir. We don't know what to do. And we haven't eaten since yesterday. There is no more food in the house.'

The hair on my arms and neck stood. A chill wound down the back of my neck and shoulders, even as it rose up to the top of my head. This was bad.

'Sir, he said he was going to kill me with his sword, Sir.'

And with that, we went from bad to worse.

Hasan Ali and Me

Part Four

If Hasan Ali and I were a three-act play, we were now at the point of confrontation.

I waited for Rahman to calm down.

'He has a sword?' I asked.

'Yes. He showed it to us a few days ago when he demanded money from us.'

If this was true, its irony was not lost on me. A sword is a scheduled weapon under The Corrosive and Explosive Substances and Offensive Weapons Act 1958 ('the Act'). The mere possession of a scheduled weapon is an offence under Section 7 of the Act. It also carries a minimum of five and a maximum of ten years of imprisonment. The provision also covers manufacturing, selling, promoting, hiring, lending, or giving of a scheduled weapon, and regards all those as offences.

'We'll deal with our present situation in a while. But first, I want to ask you about Hasan Ali. What happened after I introduced him to you?'

'He was not a problem in the first month. Everything was okay. We weren't friends, but said hello and goodbye to each other. However, in July, one day, he came home drunk. And since then, he drinks every day. More and more. He would ask us for money on the pretext that it was your order to collect more money from us. At first, we gave in, but then it began to happen every two to three days. That's when we drew a line and said no. Then, he started to punch and kick us when we didn't give him money.'

'My god, Rahman. Why didn't you call me or ask? You have my number.'

'Yes, but he is your staff. So, at first, we believed him. We didn't want to bother you, so we tried to handle it ourselves. But before we could do anything, he took away our phones. Sir, we need your help to go back to the apartment and get our things back. We didn't take anything with us when we fled. We just ran straight here.'

'How come three of you did not take him on?'

'We are not fighters, Sir. He is aggressive and seems experienced in fighting. We can't afford to get injured, Sir—we've already missed a few work days and we are worried we'll lose our jobs.'

'How did you manage to get out?'

'I told him we needed to eat. We were starving and hadn't eaten in a day. Since there was no food in the house, he let us out for half an hour, but we are supposed to go back after we eat.'

'Seriously?! You are not going back. First, get something to eat, then go stay somewhere safe for a while. I will try to speak to him and get him to leave. Come back here in the evening so we can discuss how to get your things back and what to do about him. Before you go, Rahman, I want to apologize to you and your friends. I am very sorry about this. I did not know he was like that.'

'It's okay, Sir. It's not your fault but his.'

I was stunned. I admit, I felt a little better when he said that, but I still couldn't shake the uncomfortable feeling.

I gave them money for food and drink, along with some compensation. But I felt truly awful about it.

I was furious. I called Hasan Ali, but he didn't pick up the mobile phone I had given him. I called him every ten minutes for the next few hours, my anger rising like mercury in a thermometer, climbing steadily higher with every thirty minutes he did not pick up. He was supposed to carry that mobile phone with him at all times: He had infringed a ground rule. Worse still, he illegally detained, robbed, and abused Rahman and his friends; he had broken the law.

Finally, at around three o'clock, I received a call from an unknown number on my mobile. I was sitting in the current administration area of our office, ranting about the situation to Farhan.

'Boosssss…' It was Hasan Ali.

I intensified my listening to pick out the background noise, as there was some traffic in the distance. I could hear he was not in a room. He sounded drunk.

'Hasan. Why are you not on the phone I gave you?' I asked him in Malay.

'Uhhhh… Bosss. I missplaccceeed it.'

'Where are you?'

'I am in Klangggg.'

'What are you doing there?'

'I have some delivery to make here, Bosss.'

I turned to Farhan and asked him whether anyone had sent Hasan to Klang. Without skipping a beat, he responded in the negative. 'In fact, he has not been in the office for the last three days. He hasn't even responded to any of our calls. Actually, we were going to bring it up to you,' Farhan added.

If my fury were a bonfire, that reply felt like someone had thrown a full petrol tank on it.

'You lied to me, Hasan. There is no work in Klang. You have not been in the office these last three days.'

'Bosss. Bosss. I have a lot of work, Bosssss.'

'Now listen. I am giving you a direct instruction: Get back to the office right now and explain yourself. I give you until 4.30 p.m. to come here. I will hear you out. You understand?'

He laughed. 'Yah. Yah. I am busy, Bosssss. I cannot go to office.'

'You have no work there, Hasan. Things will not go well if you don't get back here by 4.30 p.m. And oh, Rahman came to see me; I know what you did to them. They told me about your sword. That is illegal, Hasan.'

Suddenly, there was no sound on the other side of the line, as if a vacuum had sucked all sound from the other end. I sensed a change of vibe over the phone.

'He is lying! He is fucking liar, a fucking cheat. Where is he? I will kill him! Bloody bastard!' he exploded.

'Never you mind him. You come back here first and we shall speak about your work before anything else.'

'Him and his friends are fuckers. Don't believe him! Rahman's a liar!' he screamed.

'Let's start with you first. I don't believe you. Are you drinking? You sound drunk.'

'No. No. I didn't drink. Did Rahman say I am drinking? Bastard! Lying bastard! It's not true.'

'Hasan, listen to me carefully. I am going to give you one last chance. You come back—'

He hung up on me.

I sent him a message on the number he had called me from, informing him that he was fired and that his license to stay at the apartment was withdrawn. He was required to vacate by 8.30 a.m. tomorrow and deliver the motorcycle, its keys, and the mobile phone to the office by 9.00. He could keep whatever I had bought him. If he failed to comply, I would take back the apartment, the motorcycle, and lodge a police report against him. He could avoid all that if he came to the office by 4.30 p.m.

4.30 p.m. came and went, and he didn't show up. I heard nothing from him. Then, about an hour or so later, I began receiving foul and vulgar messages directed at me from two unknown numbers. I suspected Hasan Ali was behind it. The messages were clumsily worded with misspellings. In one of them, he mentioned Rahman. Hasan Ali wasn't bright, if not downright dim, but that worked fine for me. The text abuse continued sporadically from those two numbers, and another came into the mix later in the evening. As my messages were not responded to, I resent them to all the unknown numbers.

Rahman and his friends arrived in the evening. I informed them that Hasan was not cooperating and that I had given him a notice to vacate by tomorrow morning. If he complied, everything would be fine. But if he did not, we would have to go in and change the locks. I promised to keep them posted on the developments. Rahman gave me his new number and left.

The next day was Merdeka Day[7], followed by Hari Raya Haji[8], and then the weekend. It would be a long, difficult, and painful goodbye if Hasan Ali didn't leave quietly.

Thankfully, we didn't register his fingerprint for the office entrance door, so someone always had to let him in. Moreover,

---

[7] Merdeka Day is held on 31 August each year. It commemorates when Malaya achieved independence from the British.

[8] This is a Muslim festival that commemorates the prophet Ibrahim sacrificing his son in obedience to Allah. It falls on the tenth day of the twelfth month according to the Islamic calendar. One of the celebratory rituals is the sacrificial slaughtering of livestock.

with the long weekend, my lawyers were away on vacation and didn't have to be troubled by the stress and drama of what I dubbed the Hasan Ali Disaster. He was my mess, so I was responsible for cleaning it up without troubling others and with as little collateral damage as possible.

I spent the rest of the evening and night monitoring my mobile phone and the office's closed-circuit cameras to see if Hasan Ali would attempt to break in. Despite receiving a few more vulgar and threatening text messages late at night, there was little else from him. It was a restless and anxious conclusion to the night.

Morning came and went with no word from Hasan Ali. At around 3.30 in the afternoon, I lodged a police complaint and met up with Rahman, his friends, and the locksmith at my office. They were hiding out at Pelangi Damansara at the time. According to Rahman, his local Bangladeshi network in Mutiara Damansara informed him that Hasan Ali had been sighted roaming the apartment blocks and around the shops late at night and in the early morning hours with a sword, looking specifically for him. This explained the anxiousness among Rahman and his friends when they turned up.

'Why do you think Hasan has it so badly for you Rahman?'

'I don't know, Sir. Maybe, it's because I am the one speaking to him, asking him questions, and talking back.'

'So, what is your job situation?'

'Oh, we were fired because we didn't turn up for work.'

'Did you explain the situation to them?'

'They don't care, Sir. They have replacements already. They told us to go away.'

None of us had been to the apartment since they ran away, so we did not know if Hasan Ali was there. As we walked over, I felt horrible and guilty about Rahman and his friends. I felt responsible for putting these young men in the company of a rogue. Hasan Ali felt nothing like the person I thought I knew. As we approached the apartment, anxiousness coursed through me like an electric shock. I began to worry about what would go down if Hasan Ali resisted. Afterall, he was the only one among the six of us who had experience with fighting.

I banged on the door when we arrived, but there was no response. Words cannot express how relieved I was to find that Hasan Ali was not home. This was as close as I had come to fighting someone.

Hasan Ali had changed the padlock to the apartment's metal door gate. The locksmith quickly got to work on it and broke it after a few minutes. When we got into the apartment, I was stunned.

He had trashed the place. The chairs and table in the living room had been overturned and lay where they had landed. Pieces of the chair and table lay scattered on the floor. The kitchen was a mess. I walked to his room and pushed open the door.

I caught a strong whiff of alcohol the moment the door creaked open. His room was completely trashed. The dressing table mirror had been smashed, with its shards scattered on the table and the floor. A half-torn Quran lay splayed on the dressing table. It was covered in bits of glass. At the top shelf of the dressing table was an open bottle of Jack Daniel's with his *kopiah* lying next to it. The mattress slouched against the wall had slashes and stabs, tufts of stuffing sticking out. The dressing table chair was in pieces on the floor, strewn together with a tangle of clothes. I opened up the closed cupboard doors and saw clumps of clothes inside. I pushed around the clothes on the floor and discovered the mobile phone I had given him.

It was still on and had some battery left. I saw the notification: 70+ missed calls. I swiped it open and tried the PIN I had set. It worked. To think he had not bothered to change the PIN after five months!

I tapped the notifications and saw my name in the missed call list. The last fifty or so were mine; the rest were from Farhan, Asim, and Aizat. No wonder he didn't respond to us at all and ditched the phone. I clicked on WhatsApp and went through his messages. Nothing sinister: apart from us, he didn't have anyone I didn't know on his phone. In fact, he hadn't added anyone to his contacts list, except his mother. But then, this was his office phone, not his private one. I clicked on the Gallery app and saw thumbnail pictures of him.

I scrolled to his earliest picture, which he had taken two weeks after joining us. He appeared uncertain and looked warily at the camera, placing himself in the middle of the frame but appearing small in the vastness of the wall behind him. I scrolled to the next batch of photos, from about a month later where he looked happier. His face was closer to the camera than before.

There were no more photos until July, when only two pictures surfaced. In them, he wore a red bandana and was shirtless. The first picture showed his side profile, and he appeared to be screaming at something in front of him off-camera. The second picture was a full frontal shot of his face, his bloodshot eyes glaring into the camera as he screamed. His face took up the entire frame.

I scrolled to the last few photos from August. They were motion-blurred pictures of him shirtless, wearing a kopiah, while appearing to scream something, his eyes bloodshot. Some were taken up close, some from an arm's length. It looked like all the pictures were taken himself: he looked like an angry, rebelling, trapped animal. I felt anger, hurt, and pain emanate from those pictures. The hair on my arms and the back of my neck stood as I studied the pictures. I swallowed hard. *What happened to you, Hasan Ali?*

I pocketed the phone and checked in with Rahman and friends. They had finished gathering up their things and were anxious to leave. I asked them to help me pack up some of Hasan Ali's clothes in a bag so I could leave them outside for him. They also helped me in searching the apartment for the sword. I don't know whether to be thankful that we did not find it.

The locksmith finished replacing the doorknob and lock. He also brought a new lock for the metal gate. We locked up, left his bag of clothes outside the apartment, and departed.

I secured the phone and the apartment. Once I had the motorcycle, it would be a checkmate for Hasan Ali.

It was time to close down the first iteration of the Second Chance Initiative, which hadn't just been a failure, but an unmitigated disaster. Hasan Ali and I had one final act to go before we concluded our three-act play:

Resolution.

Hasan Ali and Me

Part Five

Rahman agreed to help me secure the return of my motorcycle and asked his Bangladeshi network of informers around the Mutiara Damansara area to remain on high alert for Hasan Ali. I gave him a spare set of bike keys. The plan was to wait for Hasan Ali to show up and snatch the motorcycle back from him with this spare bunch.

However, there was no sight or sound of Hasan Ali the next day around Mutiara Damansara; though he continued to send me insults, taunts, and threats from new and unknown numbers throughout the day. I did not respond, sitting riveted to my mobile phone, watching the CCTV on my office front door and checking in with Rahman for updates. It was impossible to do anything else. There was no peace of mind knowing Hasan Ali could easily move around.

Later, our maid informed us that sometime in the afternoon, he had tried to come to our house. But, much to my surprise, he had been chased away by our neighbourhood security guard, whose role I had always considered to be a mere formality. I developed a newfound admiration for him for chasing Hasan Ali away!

However, the following morning, Hasan Ali broke into the apartment, ripping the entire grill frame door off the wall and smashing the door handle to barge in. According to Rahman, Hasan Ali hadn't emerged since then. Meanwhile, one of Rahman's friends retrieved my motorcycle using the spare keys and brought it back to my house before lunch.

This was a checkmate for Hasan Ali. I texted him.

'Hasan, I have my motorcycle back. You broke into my apartment, committing another offence. I don't want to see, hear, or smell you in this area anymore. You have two hours to leave and never return, after which, I will lodge a police report against you for breaking in. If you're still around, I will have you arrested. You disappointed me, Hasan. Goodbye.'

Two hours later, I went down to police station to lodge the report and walked over to the apartment where Rahman and his friends lived. The ripped-off metal grill door leaned stiffly against the wall, while the inside door was slightly ajar. The handle hung limply, with its insides dangling out. I pushed it open and called out.

No one responded. The apartment was empty. Hasan Ali was gone, and only the mess he made remained.

I offered Rahman and his friends a rent-free, year-long stay at the apartment, even suggesting they keep the money in case they wanted to rent out one of the rooms. They accepted the proposal, and I was grateful. Though I warned them to be prudent and stay away for a week, just in case Hasan Ali returned yet. If he didn't—it was unlikely he would—the place was theirs.

They moved in a week later. On 28 March 2018, I obtained a court order to withdraw myself as Hasan Ali's surety and revoke the good behaviour bond. An arrest warrant was issued for him. Since then, I have not seen or heard of Hasan Ali, even though he sent me threat messages a day or two after leaving, but went silent eventually.

And he has been silent ever since.

With Hasan Ali gone, I put an end to my Second Chance Initiative.

Postlude

Even if its end was anticlimactic, I am nonetheless grateful, for I had enough stress over those four days to last me a year. I hadn't expected Hasan Ali to comply so meekly in the end. Despite his absence, my anger at him burned for a while, but cooled after some time.

Occasionally, I reflect on the entire episode to try and understand why Hasan Ali couldn't grasp the opportunity when it presented itself. Why did he self-destruct like that? I also narrate this tale to others to gauge if I could have dealt with the situation better or differently.

The first thing I admit is my naiveté and simple-mindedness about reform and rehabilitation. I suppose I expected a miracle to happen: present an opportunity to someone of a deserving circumstance, and voilà! I treated Hasan Ali like a reasonable man on the MRT (mass rail transit). The problem was Hasan Ali didn't take the MRT. He was a fish out of water with us. I was hoping for it to be a matter of acclimatization. Sometimes it is, sometimes it isn't.

Secondly, I didn't sufficiently consider and investigate Hasan Ali's mental and psychological state, overlooking how his experience in prison or the situation at home would have affected him. If there is one thing I can say about Hasan Ali, it is that there was a sense of something broken inside him. We are all battered and bruised in some way or other, but his cracks ran deep. My mind would return to the pictures he had taken of himself on the mobile phone. I think they were a metaphor for the deterioration of his mental condition, as the violence in his pictures mirrored the measure of his pain and suffering, further frustrated by his inability to express them articulately.

What he perhaps needed, in addition to the opportunity he was given, was to be psychologically examined and treated. I think anyone who has served some time in a lock-up or prison should go for mental counselling. While I have not been there myself, but from speaking to people with experiences of it, my sense is that they all suffer trauma: Some degree of post-traumatic stress disorder, among other things. The only question is how much. Even if they don't admit it, it is visible in their eyes, their resigned smile, and the forlorn look. Just because it's not expressed, doesn't mean it doesn't exist.

Or perhaps complete freedom was not what Hasan Ali needed.

Recently, my colleague Asim took over a criminal trial from me. It was a simple case I had initially undertaken as an opportunity to work together with my pupils. However, the trial was delayed for so long, that by the time the case came up, they had completed their pupillage and were practicing associates. Hungry for some criminal action, Asim offered to take over.

It was an absurd case of drug possession. Our client was charged with five others in connection with a common intention to possess 0.4 grams of marijuana. I joked that his defence was that there was not enough dope to go around for six people. Asim prepped for the case, only for the charge to be withdrawn. While waiting for the trial, he spoke with the client's father and discovered our client was detained under a Prevention of Crime Act[9] order ('POCA Order').

Given the father's narrative, Asim detected procedural flaws with the POCA Order. He questioned him about whether they wanted to challenge it. To his surprise, both of them refused. The father said his son was doing better there and seemed calmer. Our client, in turn, instructed us not to challenge the POCA Order, saying he preferred the

[9] Act 297 Malaysia Federal Legislation. Available at: https://lom.agc.gov.my/act-detail.php?act=297&lang=bit (Accessed: 16 December 2024).

structured life there, strict though it may be. It is what he needed, he said. This was unexpected.

When Asim told me about this, Hasan Ali came to my mind. Perhaps Hasan Ali needed rigidity and structure in his life, which we couldn't provide: Something like the army or a job where he was kept physically occupied and out of mischief. Or, perhaps, we need a system that tries to understand that each person, be it Hasan Ali or Asim's client, needs to be rehabilitated and reformed, instead of being damned to imprisonment, whipping, fines, and expecting them to become better citizens from such treatment. I have long thought that Malaysia's sentencing and reformative processes urgently need creativity, reform, and intent.

But that takes a lot of time, effort, and money, which nobody wants to spend on a convict because they are written off for life, regardless of whether it's their first or fifth offence. There is not enough money to buy them decent food, never mind a mental health consultation.

The more I reflected on Hasan Ali, the more my anger substituted itself with melancholy and ideas. He wasn't a bad man, just a flawed one, unable to get a grip on his own demons and transcend his circumstances. There are many like him in our society; it is simply a question of degree, context, and reward. In fact, many of them are rewarded for succumbing to their demons.

Despite how things came to pass between Hasan Ali and me, I hope he has found some strength to hold tight to that bit of torn opportunity that remains in his grip. I hope he has found some peace within himself to create peace outside of himself. I hope he can find some good people to be with and find happiness or contentment in his life. At the end of the day, Hasan Ali and I are not so different because, despite all our differences, I'd like to think we still want the same things out of life.

'People Like Us Never Win'

A pervasive attitude among my criminal legal aid clientele, especially those with previous convictions, is that they will always lose against the police.

Even when they choose to defend the charge, they lack the confidence to win; it doesn't matter if they committed the crime or not. The criminal justice system to them isn't about right and wrong, but those with power or money and those without. They are acutely aware of their perceived status as impecunious society outcasts up against the awesome machinery of the state.

They—mere drug addicts, sex workers, and previously convicted thieves, many of whom have often not even made it past primary school—are up against the police force, the forensics unit, the Attorney General's Chambers, civil society (when public witnesses are involved). Sometimes, they also contend with the bias of the presiding judges, who are learned and trained for their speciality. Then there are judges who are so pro-prosecution, that a trial becomes simply a waiting period before they declare the conviction and sentence. You may raise doubts that raise the dead, but it will all often come to nought.

These convicts have few to no family or friends. The only thing these outcasts have, the only thing they can rely on, is the sole pro bono lawyer defending them. It's like David with two hands tied behind his back against several fire-breathing, multi-headed Goliaths.

I used to think those with previous convictions and jail time would not deem it a big deal—a once bitten, twice shy sort of a thing. A case that challenged this assumption was a drug charge against two women and a man.

Both women had previously been convicted for engaging in sex work and drug-related charges, although only one was in recovery at the time of their arrest. The other had managed to kick the habit and was trying to reconcile with her daughter, whom she had left with a friend earlier. The man, on the other hand, was your typical drug addict working just enough to afford his next hit. At the time of arrest, he was spaced out on his latest high in a room rented from the drug dealer who owned the place.

Although they were found in different rooms at the time of arrest, all three were jointly charged with possession of a bag of drugs found in a room at the end of the hallway. They claimed that the room belonged to the drug dealer who owned the house.

While interviewing them about the facts, one of the ladies (paraphrased and translated for clarity) said, 'From your questions, I know you don't believe us because we have been convicted before. I know you think we are not good people, that is okay, but I tell you those drugs were not ours. I cannot even make ends meet. How will I afford so many drugs? Just because we are prostitutes or drug addicts doesn't mean we are lying. If we do something, even if it's bad, we will admit it. You can look at our previous convictions. We pled guilty to all of them. But those drugs, I swear to you, are not ours.'

And they did tell the truth. At the end of the prosecution's case, they won. Their story, briefly, was as follows.

They each rented a room from the drug dealer, who was getting high. One of the ladies was attending to a customer, while the other was cooling her heels, waiting to pick up her daughter a few hours later. Early in the morning, the police raided the house unannounced. Although the house was full, only three of them were caught in the raid. Naturally, they were charged for the bag of drugs found in the house.

The prosecution's story went as follows:

The lead raiding officer surreptitiously climbed up to the first-floor ledge, and through an unobscured window, he spied them 'chasing the dragon' in the room that had the drugs bag. Upon seeing this, they announced themselves and demanded my clients give themselves up, after which the three allegedly ran out of the room. The police quickly smashed through the window, chased, and apprehended them.

The prosecution lost simply because the evidence didn't support the case. The story was riddled with inconsistencies. What clinched the win was the investigating officer's evidence claiming he didn't find any drug utensils in the house. This blatantly contradicted the lead arresting officer's account that my clients fled the room and left the drug utensils on the floor.

After the verdict was announced, I didn't immediately turn back to congratulate my clients. As I mentioned, since they had multiple previous convictions (at least two each), I thought an acquittal was not a big deal for them. I gathered my belongings, tied up my file and only turned to address them after I finished.

To my surprise, they were crying and hugging each other. After congratulating them, I asked the reason behind their tears. The more outspoken of the two ladies summed it up. 'We cannot believe the court decided in our favour,' she said. 'People like us never win against the police. Never in our dreams did we think we would win. We still cannot believe we can walk out after this.'

I shook their hands, cautioned them against wanting to see their names on the Legal Aid Centre list the next time, and wished them a better life.

The Sure Win Case

'Sitters' are what I call sure-win cases.

I don't often get sitters. In fact, I rarely get them.

But that's fine with me. Usually, I prefer not to do sitters. If I take them up, I would be doing straightforward debt claims, such as credit card and housing loan, orders for sale, etc. I don't like those sure-lose cases too, which I call 'shitters'.

On the regular, I prefer cases where the chances are either 50/50, 60/40, 70/30, even 80/20, and anything in between. The chances of success or failure are uncertain. I call them the 'ambi'. 'M-Bees', plural.

To be clear, when I say sitter, loser, and ambi, I refer to our expectations of success as legal practitioners given the facts, the law, the client, the court, the opponent, the opposing litigant, etc. These terms do not refer directly to the chances of success.

The certainty of a sitter or a loser makes it uninteresting and tedious. It's like watching a movie where we know the ending. Maybe we've even seen it before entirely. Whatever the case, we're just going through the motions to reach that obvious end. Most litigants tend to believe their case is the winning one.

Having said that, running a sitter is potentially more anxiety-laden compared to a loser. The worry arises not because I think our arguments are unassailable, but because

I can't see any viable or plausible counterargument. I can't detect any flaws or any downsides in my sitter of a case either, making it feel like being unwilfully blinded.

Apart from anxiety, there is also a sense of dread about it. If the client and I agree that their case is a sitter, then our mutual expectations are of a sure win. But this is litigation, where nothing is certain. So, the possibility of losing a sitter is omnipresent, which no lawyer wants.

Shitters are the easiest of the lot because there is no expectation to win. No expectation translates to no pressure, which ultimately manifests into no anxiety and lesser stress. It is great if we win, for we'll be lauded as Houdini the magician or a miracle worker. If we lose, well, that's what we expected, isn't it? What else does one want? But be warned: Sometimes, sitters are shitters in disguise.

There was a sitter I enjoyed several years back.

It was a criminal appeal. I was appointed by the Court of Appeal to oppose the prosecution's appeal against the acquittal of the accused of a drug trafficking charge in the High Court. After reading the record of appeal, I knew I had a sitter. I'd even call it a sumo sitter of a case.

That's how confident I felt about the odds of my success.

Here are the facts: My client and another person, who was never found, had been in a delivery van that stopped outside a house somewhere in Selangor. The other missing person drove, while my client sat upfront with them. He was not part of the delivery service but had hitched a ride with the one who drove, who was an acquaintance.

Immediately after they stopped at the house, they were ambushed by a police squad waiting nearby. The driver, who had a limp, managed to escape somehow. Instead, my client, who was able-bodied, was caught. According to the arresting officer, the driver ran into a nearby forest. Despite the police giving chase, the driver outran and evaded the entire squadron because of the forest cover. If it were not for the forest, they would likely have caught him.

The High Court dismissed the case at the end of the prosecution's submissions, known to lawyers as the *prima facie* stage (Latin for 'at first blush'). The investigating officer sketched a plan of the crime scene that showed the area, where my client was arrested, as a fully developed housing area. There was no forest nearby at all.

While the court is always willing to accept a certain degree of inaccuracy by a witness, it is less forgiving about a bald lie. You can't be wrong about the existence of a forest. You just can't.

Understandably, in the written judgement, the High Court judge criticized the arresting officer and concluded that he lied in his evidence. The judge also raised serious doubt over the police squadron's competency: How did they fail to arrest the driver with a limp but managed to capture the healthy passenger instead? The judge's written grounds were emphatic, damning, and unforgiving.

To this day, I wonder why the prosecution had bothered to appeal for such a loser, and in doing so, they delivered me a sitter. I treat such instances as legal presents to be savoured and cherished. Preparing a short-written submission for it, I cited one case as authority, feeling it was so ridiculously obvious that I shouldn't even be called upon to submit.

On the day of the hearing, a petite, timid, and deferential-looking lady came up to me and introduced herself as the DPP conducting the appeal. Her face was tense, and there was a sense of resignation about her. I felt sorry for her, truly. It was like watching a sheep go into the slaughterhouse of its own accord.

'Encik Fahri, there are two matters I would like to raise with you. Do you have some time?' she asked me.

'Yes, of course. What's up, Puan?'

'Firstly, this is our written submission. I am sorry I am serving it late. It . . . it was challenging to prepare.'

'Don't worry. I completely understand.'

'I hope you won't object to my late service.'

'No worries, Puan. I won't.'

'Thank you. The second is, I intend to make an oral amendment to the date in the notice of appeal. The date of conviction is incorrect. I know it's not a big deal, but I must correct it.'

'Of course not, Puan. I won't object. Small matter. You can tell the court that for both matters.'

'Thank you, Encik Fahri.'

She nodded and whisked herself back to her seat.

We were third or fourth on the list. When our turn came, the prosecutor got to her feet. She made the application to amend the notice of appeal and apologized to the court for filing her submission late. Then, she began her oral submission.

'My Lords, this is an appeal from the . . .'

The chairing judge decided to spare us the formalities of a hearing and cut to the chase.

'Counsel, why did chambers appeal this decision?'

Boom, baby. I mini-fist-pumped at that. After hearing it, I felt my chances of being called on to respond went from likely to extremely low.

'Yang Arif? Why?'

'Yes. Why? Did you read the High Court decision?'

'Yes, Yang Arif.'

'After reading it you still want to appeal?'

'Yang Arif, if I can take you to . . .'

'No, no. The High Court judge said the arresting officer was lying, that there was a forest that the driver ran into. But the investigating officer's sketch plan shows it was a housing area. There was no forest! Did you read it or not?'

'Yes. My instructions are to appeal.'

'Instructions from your superiors?'

'Yes.'

'The judge said it was unbelievable the driver with the lame foot could escape but the healthy passenger was caught. I agree. How did that happen with what seven, eight policemen in the raid?! What were they doing? This is not explained. Are your seniors aware of this? These are finding of facts, you know?'

'Yang Arif, if I can . . .'

'Chambers shouldn't waste the court's time with these kinds of appeals. What do you expect to achieve? The arresting officer lied. It's a finding of fact. Your case is over. Please tell your superiors to not appeal for cases like this. Don't simply file frivolous appeals. Consider the judgment thoroughly and properly before doing so. We see no merit in this appeal. Eh, where is the respondent's counsel?'

I stood up immediately.

'I am here, My Lord.'

The chairing judge turned to me. He lowered his glasses.

'Ah, we don't need to hear you. This appeal is dismissed. Thank you. Next appeal.'

The prosecution did not appeal against the Court of Appeal's decision.

Losing My First Death Sentence Appeal

In my thirties, despite having a clutch of capital punishment trials under my belt and arguing matters in the Court of Appeal, I had not yet made any capital punishment appeals at the Federal Court.

That changed one afternoon, when a letter from the Court of Appeal invited me to be the appointed counsel for a drug trafficking appeal, which was against conviction and sentence.

My client was a Malay man in his late-forties. I'll call him Mat. He was tall and big, a light-browned skin giant. The soft lines on his face had not yet hardened, despite serving about four years in jail when I met him.

Mat was charged for owning a bag of drugs found in the boot of his car. The prosecution's case was that Mat had sent his car to a workshop for service around noon, where he was recognized by two workers who spotted him returning around five in the evening with a bag. They also saw him put it in the boot of his car, but didn't see the compartment in which Mat placed it. Mat left the workshop and returned at about 7.30 to pick his car up. On his way home, he was caught at a roadblock.

His defence at trial of non-exclusive possession failed in the High Court. The workshop workers' evidence placed him with the bag of drugs and the car. High Court found possession as a matter of fact and presumed trafficking, which set Mat up for a mandatory death penalty.

When I met Mat, he had already been schooled by his Kajang inmate brethren[10] about the ins and outs of criminal procedure, the evidence, and their respective offences. He spoke with a certain degree of legal acuity about the arguments that could be taken, knowing every little fact and every argument that could support his case. He knew them all by heart, and they still glowed with hope for him.

This was not going to be an uphill task, but a vertical concrete wall ten miles up.

There was an error in the grounds of judgment about when he returned to the workshop. The trial judge incorrectly wrote that Mat went back at 7.30 instead of 5.00 in the evening. It seemed to be a typo, however, the judge did not correct the judgment, which meant my client could only have gone to the workshop twice, not thrice, as alleged by the prosecution. Since the second time was 7.30, he couldn't have placed the bag there at 5.00 p.m.

But, to be fair, reading the judgment as a whole, it was clear the judge made a typographical error and accepted the workshop worker's evidence. My appeal was simply that my client be granted the benefit of doubt regarding the typo and have his conviction reduced from drug possession with enhanced sentences, which carry heavy imprisonment and whipping, to a simple possession charge. I wasn't hoping for an acquittal; instead, it was simply a device to get him off death row.

If you find this argument lame, I understand. However, something is better than nothing, especially in a death penalty

---

[10] Kajang Prison serves as the main prison and is the headquarters of the Prison Department.

case. To plead guilty or concede would be a sure shot death sentence. In some cases, challenging the charge merely delays the inevitable, as was the case with Mat.

I don't vividly remember the Court of Appeal hearing, except that it was short, intense, and ended with Mat's appeal being dismissed and his death sentence being upheld. However, to my surprise, Mat asked me to continue as his counsel for his appeal in the Federal Court. Since we lost, I had expected him to sack me and appoint another counsel, but he said he liked my spirit.

So, we went to the Federal Court. The hearing, again, was short and intense. But this time, I pushed the point much harder than I did at the Court of Appeal—not necessarily for an acquittal, but to have the charge reduced to that of possession. I tried to stress as much as possible on the typographical error, like a child riding a rocking horse. Sadly, the court didn't rule in our favour and dismissed Mat's appeal.

I immediately felt weary, and a great sadness took over me.

Although I had handled plenty death penalty trials, losing an appeal at the Federal Court bore a sense of irreversibility and finality to a person's fate. *Now, my client will die*, I thought to myself. I had failed to prevent his execution.

That's how I felt in that moment. I was miserable. I knew the facts didn't support Mat, so did he. Despite knowing there was little I could do about it, I somehow felt it was my fault. Facing Mat felt embarrassing. What could I tell him? He already knew the appeal had been dismissed, and that all I could offer him was my sympathy. What good was that?

Even though I could make the distinction that I didn't send him to death, I still couldn't not help but feel bad about it, like a bystander witnessing a horrific road accident.

Gathering my files, I forced myself over to Mat in the dock. He seemed so small sitting there.

'Hi Mat. I am very sorry that our appeal was dismissed. I wish I could have done better.' I said.

'Nothing to be sorry about, Encik Fahri. You did your best. That's all you could do.'

'Yes, but I lost. I felt we deserved, at least, a drop in charge to that of possession. I am sorry, Mat. I should have at least bagged you that.'

'No, no. Thank you for doing your best on my appeals. I know I put a lot of pressure on you, but I know it wasn't an easy case to win.' He patted me on the shoulder while being led out of the dock, handcuffed.

'It's okay. I am satisfied with how you argued my case,' he assured again. 'That is why I asked you back for this appeal. You got *semangat*[11]. Keep it going. Don't blame yourself. What is done is done.'

He was then led to the holding cells below the Putrajaya Palace of Justice[12].

And that was the last I saw him.

After being told his appeal was dismissed, effectively condemning him to death by hanging, Mat didn't get upset and miserable. Instead, he comforted his lawyer—me—over the loss of the appeal and encouraged me to keep going.

It only struck me later how composed Mat was and how utterly self-absorbed I had been then.

Since then, I have learned to deal with such losses better, due to the advice I took from a convicted drug trafficker.

---

[11] Malay for 'spirit' or 'motivation'.

[12] These are where the top two appellate courts, the Court of Appeal and the Federal Court, are located.

When Our Reputation Needs No Defence

It was a High Court court-assigned counsel case.

My client and another man—we'll call him Lan—were charged with the murder of a man.

While the prosecution alleged Lan shot and killed the victim, my client faced charges under the doctrine of common intention for a murder. This meant that even though he didn't pull the trigger himself, he could still be charged with murder because he had an alleged shared intent to commit or support or facilitate the crime.

Before the trial, having considered the prosecution's pre-trial disclosed evidence, our client's narrative, and the direction I forecasted the prosecution's case would take, I felt there was little evidence to demonstrate common intention on our client's part. In fact, on the contrary, there was even an independent witness whose testimony appeared favourable to our client.

Our strategy, as I explained to him, was to gauge the case prosecution brought against him. This meant I wouldn't cross-question many of the prosecution's witnesses, but not that I wouldn't do anything. Instead, I'd carefully monitor the situation all along. I explained to him that I intended to focus on only two key witnesses, whose evidence, I estimated, would suffice to raise reasonable doubt about my client's common intention to murder.

Lan's counsel was a former cop turned defence counsel. He was the sort that wouldn't look out of place in an alley in a sketchy part of town where you wouldn't want to wander at night. From the get-go, he was arrogant and indifferent to me.

Halfway through the prosecution stage, seven witnesses had been called. They were formal forensic witnesses, who testified about how the other accused came to possess the homemade pistol, and had it on the day in question. As their evidence neither mentioned my client's involvement nor knowledge of the pistol, I didn't cross-question any of them. Lan's counsel, however, was on his feet for all of them. But, in my uninformed estimation, he was the kind who conflated cross-examination with examining crossly, often asking questions for the sake of it.

Around that time, my client's wife called me one night, her voice trembling from indignation and punctuated by sobs.

'Evening Puan, are you okay?' I asked.

'Sorry to call you so late, Encik Fahri. I'm so sorry to bother you so late at night.'

'That's alright. You sound like you are crying. Is everything okay?'

'I just had a fight with Lan's family,' she said.

'Oh, dear! What did you fight about?'

'They said you are not a good lawyer, that you're stupid and lazy. They also doubt if you've been doing anything at all, claiming that you never ask any questions. They fear my husband is going to lose the case, as you're a court-assigned counsel, which, to their minds, are lousy lawyers. It was also suggested that I hire a lawyer they know of, who is a former cop, and charges one hundred thousand ringgit, and hence is better than you.'

'Okay. So, what were you fighting about?'

'I defended you. I said you are a good lawyer, who knows what he is doing, Encik Fahri. I told them you are neither stupid nor lazy, without divulging our strategy, of course. How can they say that about you, Encik Fahri? It's so wrong and unfair. I was so upset when they said all those horrible things. We got into a fight about that.'

'I see. Well, Puan, let me first say thank you very much for defending me. I appreciate it.

Secondly, and more importantly, you don't need to do that. Don't defend me in front of them.'

'But why? They bad-mouthing you.'

'Puan, I'm appointed to defend your husband. My focus right now is defending him so he gets the ideal outcome. What they think of me is not important. It has nothing to do with the case,' I said.

'It is not my reputation that is on stake at the trial, but your husband's life. Let them say what they like.'

'But they are saying these bad things—'

'Let them!' I interjected. 'I'm only concerned about two people's opinions: The first is the judge because they will decide the outcome of the case—not Lan's lawyer, his family, or his friends. Let's keep our efforts focused on the case. Forget about everything else outside. Just be patient.'

'I will,' She replied.

'Good. Do you mind if I ask you something?'

'Not at all.'

'Did Lan invite your husband to use his lawyer?'

'Yes.'

'Why didn't he go with their lawyer?'

'Actually, he wanted to. Lan's family even said he wouldn't need to pay and emphasized being together. But I thought, *jap*, if they pay the fee, that would mean they get to control the lawyer and we would have no say. What if their lawyer doesn't protect my husband and instead blames him for it? Lan's story isn't the same as my husband's. I didn't feel comfortable, Encik Fahri, and insisted he take a separate lawyer. We fought about it, but after he met you, he was fine with using another lawyer.'

The instincts of my client's wife were sharp and right. After listening to her, I suspected Lan's family was happy to have my client represented by their lawyer because he could be the sacrificial lamb.

In a criminal trial, one must be wary of offers for help from a co-accused or anyone in general. The stakes are high, as nobody wants to be convicted and imprisoned for a long time. Just because you are charged with the same offence as someone else, doesn't necessarily mean your interests are aligned.

'I see,' I continued. 'That was very good advice for your husband. I'm glad you insisted on it. Now, that brings me to the other person's opinion I am concerned about: your husband. He is my client, and if he doesn't have confidence in me to fight his case, he should find another lawyer. So, does your husband have confidence in me?'

'Yes, of course, Encik Fahri. He is happy you are acting for him. He understands what you are doing.'

'Thank you, Puan. I am glad to hear that. Then, we continue with our strategy. Moving forward, avoid Lan's family.'

The defence for both the accused persons was called at the end of the prosecution's case.

Lan's counsel called me up a month before the defence's trial. He pleaded me to change my client's story to match his. I politely declined. By then, his client was damned. All the witnesses had also pinned the gun on him. There wasn't any evidence to infer common intention against my client either. I even managed to elicit favourable evidence from my targeted witnesses.

After that, Lan's counsel called me several times, despite being rebuffed each time.

At the end of the defence, my client was acquitted.

Lan was convicted and sentenced to death. He later lost all his appeals in the appellate courts. The prosecution also dropped the case against my client after we successfully defended his acquittal in the Court of Appeal.

After the decision was announced, I told my client to be grateful to his wife for advising him to get his own lawyer. The outcome might have been very different if he had not listened to her. And that when it came to deciding important matters, he best defer to her.

Before leaving the courtroom, I passed the other guy's family in the gallery. On the way out, I glanced at them: they looked sad, disappointed, and frustrated. As I passed, they turned to look at me.

I felt the heat of their silent stare warm my back as I walked out of the courtroom.

The Time a Client Conned Me

I don't expect much gratitude from my legal aid clients. Not that I don't care for it, but it would be unfair to do otherwise. It is enough they shake my hand and thank me for my efforts when I am done, which most of them do anyway. It feels good when they give a thumb-up. Occasionally, a meal is strongly insisted upon, and if I have the time, I oblige.

Then, there are those utter cads.

This one, in particular, was a costly lesson.

In my early days of practice, I was appointed to act for a man and his wife. He was one of those emasculated-looking security guards, with a rifle slung around their thin bodies, dressed in a uniform two sizes bigger sitting meekly outside a small supermarket, toll, or jewellery shop. The woman was a housewife, though I never met her.

They used to live in a squatter area in Kuala Lumpur, after which they were relocated and allocated an apartment. In order to purchase it, they were given a monthly instalments-loan by a government-affiliated finance company.

On paper, his pay would be able to cover it, but it would be tight: no small change even. At home, he had a healthy, strapping son, who was in his early twenties. However, he neither studied, nor did anything productive, except occasionally turn up for meetings. Once, I questioned the man that why he didn't ask his young and healthy son to work, as he was already in his early sixties. 'He doesn't listen to me', the man replied.

When I was appointed as their lawyer, the family was being evicted from his apartment owing to a serious loan default, for which a judgment had been obtained against them. An auction resulted in the sale of their apartment to an individual, whom I'll refer to as the landlord.

The landlord had signed the sale and purchase agreements, and taken legal ownership of the property. Now, he wanted to rent the place out after evicting my clients, who were of meagre education and not the type who could meticulously peruse the papers. Hence, they had ignored all the legal notices, thinking the situation would improve. They finally woke up when we were at the tail end of the whole process of legal ownership transfer.

I asked him whether he could vacate the house and put up with any of his family members. Only one relative offered room and board, he replied, for six hundred ringgit per month. In the meantime, I negotiated a rental deal with the landlord at six hundred fifty ringgit per month. However, my client couldn't afford either. After accounting for the necessities, he didn't even have a hundred left. It also meant they had no money to pay for filing, affirmation, search, etc. They were too broke to move or to stay.

When I looked closer into the auction proceedings, I noticed that the apartment sale had yielded an extra twenty thousand ringgit. The finance company stayed quiet about the extra amount earned from the sale and hadn't informed my client. After several notices and threats of legal action, they agreed to settle and pay them. This, however, took time, so I was doing my best to hold off the vacancy proceedings by attacking the judgment it was premised on, trying to set aside the rest of the orders obtained by the finance company and landlord.

My clients resolved to leave the place as soon as they had the money.

Once I secured the finance company's agreement to refund the money to my clients, I finished off all the other cases immediately. After much negotiation, I settled all the landlord's costs at just over a thousand ringgit. It was very generous of him, considering how much he must have had to pay his own lawyers and the trouble he endured. Apart from this, I had also advanced over a thousand more for the disbursements. When I finally brought them the cheque for the excess amount, I reminded them of these, which had to be paid immediately when they cashed it.

After they received the money, my client never came to see me or phoned me. He didn't even answer my calls. His son, who initially picked up, said his father would come to visit me soon, which went on for about two weeks until he stopped responding.

I apologized to the landlord's lawyer, whom I had assured that the money would come in once they would encash the cheque, but it didn't come through. I mirrored her frustration and told her that my client had screwed me over too.

In hindsight, I should have made the finance company hand the cheque to me, after which I would pay it out to the landlord's lawyers, reimburse myself, and refund the balance. In my naiveté and wanting to show that I wasn't short-changing them, I allowed the cheque to be made out to the man and his family. I was as angry at myself as I was at them.

That's what I got for simply assuming that my clients are trustworthy and honest. I learned that each person must be considered on their own, without any preconceptions.

Moreover, I also overlooked a basic lesson: Money should be paid to you as the lawyer first.

These two lessons cost me more than a thousand ringgit, so it's best you get them here for free!

I also knew that people who are poor, such as my clients, usually have little understanding of their legal obligations. They were squatters who had never dealt with loan payments or water and electricity bills. Upon relocation into the apartment, they had to pay for things they weren't accustomed to. They had never dealt with these issues and didn't know how to either.

Take, for instance, their obligation to pay the loan. My client claimed he paid it off; what he didn't mention was he had made a lump sum payment every time he had money, and failed to service the loan monthly, thinking he could pay as and when he had it. Even though he signed the loan agreement, his obligations were not fully explained to him. Initially, he was outraged after the bank sold his land, despite him paying the instalments, until I explained the paperwork to him.

Incidents like this suggest the government must do more to raise awareness among squatters about their new responsibilities and help them prepare for when they move into apartments. They should also be informed about all their responsibilities once they move into the allocated housing.

A few months later, I heard they moved out of their place and disappeared. I returned the file to the legal aid clinic with a request that they be blacklisted, which was allowed a few weeks later.

Lessons to Be Learned Everywhere

One of the first criminal cases I handled, circa 1999, was of a motorcycle theft charge. It also included an alternate charge involving possession of stolen property against a juvenile in the then-Juvenile Courts, where a magistrate heard and decided the case with two non-lawyers.

While I was handling the case, serendipity found me in the process of devouring the *Rumpole* series of books written by the inimitable Sir John Mortimer, who passed away on 16 January 2009. As a quick recommendation, I can't emphasize on the importance of the series enough to budding lawyers, particularly those inclined towards criminal practice. According to a legend, Amer Hamzah, one of the Malaysian Bar's most well-known criminal legal practitioners, was inspired by the *Rumpole* collection to take up his first legal aid criminal case, leading him down the criminal legal aid path. One of the stories from the series helped me appreciate the evidence that was my key to winning this case.

I forgot the name of the story, but I remember the instance of relevance vividly enough, where Rumpole defended one of his regular clients for an offence. What complicated it was a written admission his client purportedly signed admitting to the offence. Apparently, the admission was given under duress, which Rumpole had trouble proving because his client lacked credibility, owing to his frequent stints in prison. Despite this,

Rumpole found the thread that unravelled the prosecution's net. It lay in a word used in the admission statement—a slang that his client wouldn't know, but a cop would. Later, Rumpole's client was acquitted.

In my case, instead of an admission, it was a police report. According to it, the Malaysian Volunteers Corps Department (RELA) volunteers were carrying out their security rounds, when they spotted my client and his friends acting suspiciously in the motorcycle parking area. They arrested him. Upon frisking, they found keys on him, after which, they took the motorcycle, my client, and his friends down to the police station.

The entire report was fictional.

According to my client, at the time of the incident, early in the morning, he and his friends had been hanging outside one of his friend's apartments. He was on his mobile phone when some RELA volunteers turned up and questioned them rudely. The situation escalated when one of them accused my client of stealing the phone that was in his hand. There was a verbal exchange, after which the volunteers left, only to return half-an-hour later and arrest my client and his two friends, this time accusing them of stealing the motorcycle.

Naturally, the prosecution summoned the person, a RELA officer, who had lodged the police report. Interestingly, the prosecuting officer (a legally qualified cop, not a DPP) was not accurate about the facts leading up to the offence with the witness. He asked a few general questions and sought his verification of the police report.

With Rumpole's story fresh in my mind, I realized that the witness's expression in court didn't seem consistent with the report. His words and sentence structure were different, even if we account for the clash between oral and written expressions. It felt off.

I pulled at the thread. Initially not referring to the police report, I instead asked the witness to recite the facts from memory. Before he could complete, he had contradicted many of the material facts in the document. They differed so much that I was confident about accusing him of not having written the report.

However, to my surprise, he admitted to not penning it, confessing that only his name had been used for it. Then, he revealed the name of the writer.

Naturally, it was the next witness, another RELA officer. He was nervous, anxious, and worried. His demeanour suggested he didn't think he would ever be called to the witness box. The prosecuting officer had committed the same error as before, failing to guide him through the facts of the incident. He was merely asked to confirm that he had written the police report.

I applied the same approach as that of the first witness. Before long, he confessed that although he authored the report, he had taken instructions on its content from another RELA officer, who had directed the report to be lodged under the first witness's name. By this time, the Magistrate was furious. She slammed her pen down and scolded the witness for lying. It was incredibly satisfying to watch.

This was my first *direct* experience with the RELA officers, and I haven't been impressed since. In this case, three of them had tried to fix a teenager up for a crime, simply because they felt he was being disrespectful towards them. The proceedings took almost a year and a half to complete. Throughout the trial, the RELA officers and the cops would approach my client and his mother to persuade them to plead guilty.

'Sure-lose one this case,' they would say. 'Why you bother fighting? All our witnesses are RELA officers. Of course, court will believe them,' they would add among other things like these.

It got to the point where my client was taken in and wanted to plead guilty due to their incessant persuasions. As the officers would not approach them when I was around, I began to sit with them in the court. This was one good enough motivation to grill those RELA officers on the stand.

With those witnesses, it is no wonder we won the case. No prizes for guessing that the prosecution lost at the prima facie stage, meaning they were unable to prove their arguments. I informed my client's father that he could lodge a police report for perjury against the RELA volunteers, as the court records reflected their crime. However, that family was noble. Despite all they went through, they harboured no malice against the officers, wanting to merely move on with their lives. As far as he was concerned, it was over for him, he told me. He didn't want the case to disrupt his kid's life anymore.

The lesson here? Lessons can be learned everywhere. It is even better if they are found in fiction books we enjoy! This was a case of fiction influencing fact as surely as fact influences fiction. It is not surprising because both of these have the potential to lead us to the same destination—truth.

Though the stories—in this case, the witnesses'—may be fictional, but their lessons transcend that distinction.

The Time Amer Found Crime

Amer Hamzah and I took our Certificate of Legal Practice (CLP) course at the University of Malaya (UM), back in 1997-1998—the second last time they offered it. A mixture of UM lecturers and part-time practising lawyers conducted the course, who varied in quality, from the amazingly good to the indifferent and perfunctory. In quantity, the latter outnumbered the former.

Amer typically wore black, heavy metal rock-inspired, printed T-shirts with jeans to the class. Quite honestly, I thought it was rather juvenile of him. We all wore those T-shirts back in undergrad college, but now, it is post-university, dude! Who would have thought the beast he has become started off with a slim collection of fictional stories back in the day? Who would have thought he would transform into the famed, feared, fashionable, and *phowaargghr* lawyer he is today?

We remained acquaintances through CLP, acknowledging each other and chatting whenever we happened to be around each other. Outside of that, we made no special effort to hang out, as both of us, by then, had our respective friend groups.

Amer and I were the lucky few who were able to clear the CLP in the first attempt. We had filed our call papers around the same time, eventually being called within a week of each other. He pupiled at Zain & Co. while I was mentored at my father's firm. His office was just around the corner from the courts, back when they were located along Jalan Raja. Mine was in Bukit Damansara, a ten to fifteen-minute drive away, depending on traffic.

We would see each other in the lower courts or the court canteen, where most of us new and young lawyers congregated after our matters. We always found company there, along with conversation and a drink. On any given day, there was someone new to meet or catch up with. Hanging out at the canteen was the best part about going to court when we started out.

Sometime in our second or third year of practice, Amer and I bumped into each other at the airport. Both of us were flying to Alor Setar for a matter the next morning. We were on the Saturday evening flight from Subang. It also turned out, fortuitously, that we had booked rooms at the same hotel. We cabbed together after landing and agreed to catch up over dinner.

Before I relate our dinner, I need to set out three matters to provide the context to that meal.

Firstly, then and now, I believe, like a religion, that there is at least one book meant for each of us.

It speaks about our deepest yearnings, yields clues as to who we could become, or teaches us something we didn't know about ourselves. It's the book that irretrievably changes us. It doesn't have to be a famous, classic, deep, or holy book—to each our own. It is a physical book.

Each sentence recasts us until, by the end of it, we arrive at the start, having begun or completed our own Copernican revolution. Despite knowing it was written for the many, it still feels as if it were penned only for us. After that book, we do not simply feel, think, and appreciate differently; we *are* different. I wrote 'at least one book' because I believe there is more than one. There are a great many books out there that have such capacity. One of my life's quests is to discover them.

Another one of my great pleasures is to find such books and give them to those I think they are suited for, and then watch them flourish or resonate. It does not happen all the time, of course; more often than not, it doesn't click. But that's fine; if it happened all the time, there would be no sense of thrill for when it does.

But when somebody *gets* the book I give them, they are generous in their gratitude and gush over how it deeply resonated with them or blew their minds open. I derive a deep sense of satisfaction when this happens. I feel I have discharged my duty to the recipient and serendipity's cause. I like to be that guy who gives you '*dhat boohke*'.

Secondly, about a year or so earlier, I discovered Horace Rumpole, the fictional character created by John Mortimer, an English barrister and writer. Rather, I finally stopped being a tart about it and read him like every lawyer should. Many are surprised to learn that I discovered him late. I must confess: The sole reason for that is my pettiness.

Back in university, there was a geeky fellow who, even though was quite *lansi*[13], harboured great enthusiasm for Rumpole. His association with Rumpole made me feel repulsed by the character back then.

When I finally got around to reading Rumpole, I realized what that lansi fella was on about. Now, I was mad about Rumpole too! Like him, I was also fervently frothing at the mouth about it. I bought any book that had the word 'Rumpole' on it. If you stamped that name on an empty, filthy, discarded milk carton, I'd have bought it. I touted him to anyone who gave me the shadow of an opportunity. At last, I suffered the Ancient Mariner syndrome for my pettiness.

[13] Stuck-up or arrogant person.

Mortimer wrote a few stories for each Rumpole volume, which were later collected into a three-volume omnibus version. The omnibus version is easier to procure than the original, individual volumes. I prefer the latter, for they are slim and easier to carry. In the early 2000s, such books were difficult to procure in Malaysia.

Thirdly, before I go on any trip, no matter how long, I must bring a few books with me—between three and five, at least one fiction, one non-fiction, and one graphic novel. I don't aim to finish them but carry them for variety. Before I left for the Subang Jaya airport, I stood by my bookshelf, pondering whether to take with me the third Rumpole volume. I was already carrying two of its individual volumes, along with two other books. Yet, I was eyeing the slim volume of the 'best of' Rumpole.

There was no need for it—I already had two in my hands.

But, nonetheless, I reached out and grabbed it. It just felt right.

Now, back to Amer and dinner. We ate at the hotel coffee house, and it was the first time we sat down together properly for a meal in forever. We discussed the usual: our practice, our respective complaints about it, and our future plans. This was a time both of us still entertained the idea of joining the Attorney General's Chambers. Amer was pursuing civil and corporate litigation claims. He said it was okay but didn't get his heart racing. That's when I told him what I was up to for fun.

'Have you heard of the Bar Council Legal Aid Centre?'

'No,' he said.

'You should. They have a lot of cases but not enough lawyers. You can take up civil or criminal cases or both—as many as you like. It's great fun! When I turned up and asked how many can I take, their response was, "How many can you take?" I have taken civil and criminal cases. All of them are going on at the same time.'

'We can do criminal cases?' he asked. 'That sounds interesting. I have been thinking about it but don't know how to get cases. Are there any criteria to fulfil before I can take up criminal cases?'

'Nope. So long as you have a pulse, a valid practising certificate, and the desire for the criminal, you are set. There's just one downside, if you can call it that.'

'What is it?'

'There is no pay. It's all pro bono. You can claim a fifty-ringgit travelling expense, but I don't bother. If you do civil cases, you will be reimbursed for whatever advances are made for the case. But whatever costs are received should go to the legal aid centre.'

'Hiya, small matter, lah, that one. I'm more interested in doing a criminal case. I don't have any experience and would like to get some. There is no opportunity to do criminal work at my firm; they do civil work only. This sounds like a good way to get a taste of it. So, how do we go about this? Just walk down to the centre and express willingness to take up cases?'

By then, I was a frequent visitor at the Kuala Lumpur Bar Council Legal Aid Centre, or KL LAC. I frequently took up and returned cases, hung out there after finishing my court matters, and was a member of the management panel committee. I knew everyone at the centre.

'Pretty much. Speak to Mani or Chitrah,' I told him. 'Tell them I referred you and the kind of cases you want. They would happily have another lawyer on the roster to take up cases.'

We talked a bit more, then called it a night and went back to our respective rooms.

Upon my return, I reflected on my conversation with Amer. Suddenly, the image of the third Rumpole volume materialized in my mind. *Oh, wow, was that why I brought that book along?* I thought.

I grabbed the book, went over it, walked over, and knocked on the door of Amer's room. He opened the door.

'If you are thinking of doing criminal cases, you'll want to read this,' I said, handing him the slim volume of the best of Rumpole. Even though I didn't think about it then, I suppose it was the best introduction I could have given him to the character. 'I think you will like it.'

Next morning, we checked out early and headed to court together.

I don't remember what happened after that. It's all a bit hazy. But I recall Amer telling me, not long after, that he loved the book. He also confessed that he wanted to head to the KL LAC to take up criminal cases. Later, someone from there informed me that Amer dropped in and took up several criminal cases at a go.

From then on, he did not look back. He took up as many criminal cases as he could, and quickly surpassed my tally. He seemed to be addicted to criminal cases, reading or thinking up arguments all the time. In those days, he would call me up to run an argument he was hypothesizing about on weekends too. He looked like he was having the time of his life, and I was very happy for him.

Moreover, he was a Rumpole convert, having developed an annoying penchant for declaring, 'I never plead guilty!' This was Rumpole's credo, especially when we pleaded that a case had no merits.

He fought a variety of cases early in his criminal practice career, but I recall his particular interest in and eventual success with sexual offence cases. He defended many, particularly those accused of rape. In the KL subordinate circles, he began to be known as *loyar bawah pinggang*, or below-the-waist lawyer. One time, he had angered a women's groups with his submission for a rape acquittal with his infamous 'cucumber from the back in the darkroom did not prove penile penetration'[14] argument.

Moreover, his command over medical terminology, along with the knowledge of the female genitalia was so impressive that a medical officer he once cross-examined conceded he didn't know which part of the genitalia Amer was referring to, when he used medical jargon. That provoked a wry comment from the bench. 'Encik Amer, sex expert ya?' being one of them.

As was common for volunteer lawyers then, Amer was a regular at the KL LAC. Soon, in the early 2000s, he rose up the ranks to be its honorary secretary, a position I took over after him.

Shortly after, we became fast friends, enjoying pursuing cases and serving the KL LAC. If we didn't see each other in court, I would show up at his office after work for breakfast or lunch. We also handled a few legal aid cases together, which was good fun.

Amer led me on my first-ever death penalty case, something I wanted to get my feet wet with but hadn't found the temerity to shoulder the psychological burden of a guilty verdict for. Working on the case with someone who knew what he was doing was a good way to obtain experience without causing anyone harm.

---

[14] In Malaysia, in order to prove rape in court under section 376 of the Penal Code, the prosecution must establish two things, amongst others: first, that there was sexual penetration; and second, that the penetration was penile. If the prosecution fails to prove penetration was caused by a penis, it doesn't constitute rape. However, it may serve as the basis for another offence.

This was a murder case, which we lost. It didn't help that the victim's maid escaped and lived to tell the tale. Our client turned out to be a convincing liar and a cold-blooded killer.

I didn't feel bad. We did all that we could. Our client was a psychopath. It was what it was.

I remember when Amer told me he wanted to leave Zain & Co. so he could practise criminal law full-time. 'About time!' was my only reaction. Since those early legal aid days, Amer has grown in ability and stature to become a very fine criminal lawyer. Reflecting on his career trajectory, I think it is amazing how he took off with a sliver of Rumpole's best and hasn't stopped soaring since. It gives me immense delight to know I was the one to give him *dhat boohke.*

To Argue or Not to Argue?

Once, I had a dilemma. It arose when I conducted a criminal appeal in the Court of Appeal for a charge of drug trafficking, an offence punishable with death by hanging.

The appellant (a person appealing against a decision) was caught when he arrived at the Kuala Lumpur International Airport after flying in from an African country. After he cleared passport control, he was arrested because the cops found his behaviour to be suspicious: He had arrived at 9 p.m., but only went for immigration next morning at around 10 a.m. His reason? He was to meet his contact, a man nicknamed 'Boy', around that time.

The police searched his body, but it didn't yield anything. Later, he was taken to Serdang Hospital to be X-rayed, which revealed many foreign objects in his stomach. There, he was given laxatives to excrete those objects over a few days.

He excreted seventy-plus capsules, each varying between 5 centimetres and 5.5 centimetres, which weighted close to 1 kilogram, with a net weight of 600 grams of methamphetamine, commonly known as meth.

I felt sorry for the officer and the photographer who had to come to the hospital after every load the appellant excreted to mark, photograph, and document the evidence. It was, undoubtedly, a shitty job, but someone always has to do it.

They charged him with drug trafficking. In Malaysia, this is a charge under section 39B of the Dangerous Drugs Act 1952 ('DDA52'). In practice, we call this the '39B'.

The Appellant's defence was that after having asked his employer what it was, he had been persuaded to believe that what he swallowed was some African herb. His employer had explained he wished to avoid payable tax if the herbs were purchased officially. There was a hint of some duress about it. Before the appellant came to Malaysia, his employer flew him out of his country and had him stay in a different country. Once there, he was told he couldn't go home unless he first carried out this task.

I felt two plausible arguments could be made from these facts.

First, the trial judge's misapprehension of the evidence related to the appellant's knowledge of the drugs. I thought it was a fifty-fifty argument; it was on a wing and a prayer, but I wasn't sure whether it would fly. I wasn't going for a full acquittal, but hoped for a reduction of the charge to section 39A DDA52, which was punishable only with imprisonment and whipping, not death. We call this the '39A'.

39A is an offence of drug possession but with an increased penalty if the amount is over a particular threshold. Depending on the weight, the mandatory minimum sentence is that of two years and three strokes of the rotan and up to a minimum of five years and ten strokes of the rotan. We could appreciate that 39A would be the preferable sentence to 39B. But not having been through either, I am in no position to endorse one over the other.

I was less confident about the second argument—or, to be honest, I didn't think very much of it. It was that the trial judge found the appellant guilty through 'double presumptions'.

In order to appreciate what it is, I will first explain what a presumption is.

In law, a presumption is something the court can assume to have happened or exist, once a particular set of facts is proven. For example, if X is proven in court to be in a room with a bag of drugs, to which only he has the key, near him, the court will presume that he knows about the drugs unless X can prove otherwise. This is known as a 'true presumption'.

A presumption can be rebutted or challenged. In court, X has to prove their lack of knowledge about the bag's contents. The standard of proof, or SOP, has to be proven on a balance of probabilities or BOP: It was more likely to have happened than not. This is known as the 'civil' BOP because it applies to all non-criminal matters. It is a lower standard than the criminal BOP, which is beyond a reasonable doubt or BRD.

The prosecution must prove BRD that X committed an offence. This means there must be no reasonable doubts about the facts and evidence that X committed the offence before the court can convict him.

A double presumption occurs when a judge invokes a presumption because of another one. Following the earlier example, let us assume the bag of drugs contains 1 kilogram of meth. The court now presumes that X is trafficking the meth, since its amount exceeds 50 grams. Section 2 of the Dangerous Drugs Act 1952 defines the term trafficking as follows:

> 'Trafficking' is defined under the act as doing any of the following in relation to the drugs: supplying, distributing, procuring, delivering, sending, carrying, transporting, administering, storing, receiving, giving, selling, buying, concealing, keeping, exporting, importing and manufacturing.

In short, the definition covers anything that is related to drug dealing. Even if X only hides the drugs momentarily, they can potentially be charged with trafficking. The provision was meant to catch anybody and everybody involved in the act of bringing drugs into Malaysia and selling them, irrespective of their actual contribution in the drug dealing operation.

However, double presumptions are not allowed.

The Federal Court asserted so, in the decision of *Muhammad bin Hassan v PP*]1998] 2 CLJ 170. Chong Siew Fai FCJ remarked, '. . . it would be unduly harsh and oppressive to construe the automatic application of presumption upon presumption as contended by the learned Deputy Public Prosecutor – a construction that ought to be adopted only if, *upon the wordings of the two subsections, such an intention of the Parliament is clear*, which, in our opinion, is not.'

I have italicized the above phrase to show where His Lordship had suggested that a double presumption could occur only if the parliament has legislated for it. The problem for the Public Prosecutor, then, was that the Dangerous Drugs Act 1952 did not expressly permit this. Surprisingly, the government did not take the cue until 15 February 2014, when a new section, called 37A, was inserted into the Act to allow judges to use double presumptions.

The constitutionality of 37A was considered in the Federal Court in *Alma Nudo Atenza v PP & Another Appeal* [2019] 5 CLJ 780. The Federal Court struck down 37A. Richard Malanjum, CJ, in a unanimous decision, held that the provision was 'a grave erosion to the presumption of innocence housed in' Article 5(1) read with Article 8(1) of the Federal Constitution.

So, even if double presumptions are legislated for, they can't stand valid because it is unconstitutional. In other words, you cannot apply double presumptions.

Coming back to the case. I wasn't confident about the double presumption argument because, having read and re-read the record of appeal several times, it seemed clear to me that the trial judge had made a finding of actual possession first and only then invoked the presumption of trafficking, which was proper and as per law. Even though there was some ambiguity about what the trial judge's remarks halfway through her decision, by the end of her judgment, it was clear that she hadn't used double presumptions to convict my client.

While both arguments were included in our written submission, I felt confident only about the first argument. I considered it over the weekend and decided to just go with the first issue. I felt that if I couldn't even pretend to convince myself, I would not be able to fool the bench. Moreover, why waste all our time on it? I decided it was going to either be the first argument, or nothing.

That day, the bench of judges was eerily quiet. There was hardly any interruption to my submission of the first argument. It had been a while since I had appeared before such a passive bench, hence it felt strange to just go on and on without even a remark. Upon concluding my first argument, I sat down.

Finally, the court stirred to life.

'Counsel, don't you have another argument to canvas?' asked the chairing judge.

In my mind, I had removed the second argument entirely, thinking there was only one argument.

'Not today, My Lord,' I replied.

'Your written submission mentions two arguments. But you have only canvassed one.'

'Ah, yes. I don't intend to canvas that, My Lord. I will leave that for my written submission.'

'Considering the charge your client is facing, shouldn't you advance every argument in his favour?'

'Yes. But for myself, I will put forth only those I think have a reasonable chance of success. There are too many holes in that argument, My Lord. I think the High Court made it quite clear at page forty-five of her ladyship's grounds of judgment: There was a finding of actual possession before invoking the presumption of trafficking.'

Suddenly, a voice came from my left. The judge seated to the right of the chair stirred.

'But what about what the judge wrote at page twenty-three?'

Ironically, the judge used the arguments in our submission to argue that the trial judge had applied a double presumption. Although, I batted them away easily enough. *What a hilarious position to be in,* I thought, *I'm arguing against my own argument!*

After the judges finished asking questions, I informed the court that I would make my submission about the issue, since they were interested. I made my submission in five minutes, referencing the Federal Court's decision of *Alma Nudo Atenza v PP & Another Appeal* [2019] 5 CLJ 786, concluding that double presumption cannot apply. The judge had done this on page so and so of her judgment, and in doing so, the learned judge misdirected herself in law.

Then, I sat down.

I confess I was taken aback at the judge's suggestion that I should advance any and every argument in favour of my client. It prompted me to wonder: Do I advance all arguments, irrespective of their plausibility? Or should I only argue those I think are plausible enough for the court to accept, and hopefully decide for in my favour?

To argue every point or to be discerning?

I am of the latter school of thought: I present only the arguments that I find plausible. I felt this accorded with my experience and reading that judges are usually not impressed by the number of arguments raised but rather appreciate counsel that is cogent, interesting, and ideally limited to three main arguments, wherever possible.

I could have raised many silly and petty arguments that might have satisfied the criteria of 'arguments in favour of my client' in that appeal. However, ultimately, if nothing appealed to them, what was the point? It was akin to winning a battle, but losing the war. As court officers, we are obliged to use the court's limited time respectfully and economically. It would be a disservice to the courts and the general public to waste its time with implausible and ineffective arguments.

Peter Lyon counsels this in his book *Advocacy: A Practical Guide.*[15] I share Nigel Pascoe QC's thoughts on this:

> The starting point is the preparation of your Grounds of Appeal. You must be absolutely ruthless in paring them down to the minimum. Leave out those half points, often minor issues of fact. They will haunt you before an unimpressed Court and they damage your credibility.[16]

Jason L. Honigman articulates this in greater detail in his article 'The Art of Appellate Advocacy':[17]

> In planning a brief, one may be confronted with a number of available arguments that vary considerably in their degree of persuasiveness. In deciding which arguments to use, one may well accept the precept that if the strongest points are unlikely to result in victory, then there is very little chance whatever of winning the case. By limiting the argument to the strongest points, one adds emphasis to those points

[15] Wildy, (2019) Simmonds & Hill Publishing; p. 208, paragraph 5.4.

[16] Pascoe, N. (2018) in Advocacy Plus: A Guide For Young Advocates. PublishNation, p. 50.

[17] Michigan Law Review (1966) Vol 64, pp. 1055–1068.

> and avoids the danger of diverting the court's attention. Moreover, the lesser arguments, when unacceptable to the court, may create the erroneous impression that the case depends on an argument which is intended only as an added buttress. Finally, a judge's rejection of a subsidiary argument may color his impression of the soundness of the whole brief.

Honigman also notes that many capable lawyers have disagreed with this view, believing that all available arguments and issues must be used. Their rationale being, since a lawyer cannot be sure which arguments will convince the court, they should advance all of them.

I find this view to be grounded more in theory and self-interest than in practice. To believe that we, as lawyers, are incapable of evaluating the merit of an argument is nonsensical. We *constantly* evaluate evidence, facts, and the law for their utility and value—repeating the same for arguments. I cannot help but think it is a complete waste of the court's time to advance arguments that, to our mind, have little to no chance of being accepted. That is why the plausibility criteria is important, and an honest assessment of it is a lawyer's duty and responsibility.

After ruminating the judge's remarks, I must confess I was shaken but, thankfully, not stirred.

The attending DPP, did not grasp the first argument, which the bench attacked him on. After ten minutes, they concluded that there was only so far they could have travelled in that car, and that they had gotten out after ten minutes. I was asked if I had anything to say in response. I replied that I didn't believe there was any argument worth addressing further and had nothing to submit, unless the court requested it. The bench reserved its decision for about forty-five minutes and then gave a short oral judgment.

They agreed with my first argument, deciding that the trial judge had misdirected herself regarding the facts. However, since the Appellant was found in actual possession of the drugs and the evidence for it was overwhelming, the conviction under 39B remained intact. Although the trial judge's reasoning was flawed, her decision, ultimately, was correct. The bench did not mention my second argument, and the appeal was dismissed.

I left the court with a niggling sense that I deserved a 39A, given the court had agreed with my first argument. I didn't deserve a full dismissal or acquittal. It felt as though I had come close, yet fallen so far away.

However, I acknowledged that the court's decision was reasonable, given the facts.

On my way out, I met the African interpreter for the case. He introduced himself and congratulated me on my argument, which left me puzzled.

After introducing myself, I asked, 'Why do you congratulate me?'

'Because the court agreed with you.'

'Yes, but we still lost.'

'Oh, that is not your fault! It is very difficult for those who swallow drugs to win. You made a good argument, and they agreed. That is the best you can do. I have never seen anyone win when drugs are found in their stomach.'

He smiled, patted me on my shoulder, and walked off.

The Death Penalty

I have never liked this question because it demands an answer that is absolutely binary.

It is either a yes or a no, with nothing in between. There is no room for an explanation because none is asked for.

It is a question that intentionally excludes the possibility of nuance.

If I am in no mood to argue, I will say I'm against the death penalty.

If I am in the mood, and ready for it, I will tell them what I really think.

And what I really think is that death penalty should be reserved for only the most heinous of crimes by the most irredeemable offenders.

So, yes, it should be retained. But for an exclusive class of criminals.

An example of such an offender is a serial killer. Those who have killed many, who derive a deep pleasure from the pain, harm, violence, and death they inflict upon others, and who are so set in their murderous, evil, and vile ways that there is no hope of reform. Those so immune to conventional punishment that it can't achieve any of the purposes of sentencing: rehabilitation, retribution, deterrence, denunciation, and protection of the community.

I think the present death penalty offences should be replaced with prison sentences for first-time offenders. If there is a second conviction for a similarly serious offence, the judge can consider applying death penalty. The third time would still be the judge's discretion, but it would, then, weigh in favour of death.

What I described above would apply to the present death penalty offences such as murder, abetment of suicide of a child or insane person, attempted murder while under a life sentence, kidnapping or abducting to murder, hostage taking resulting in death, rape resulting in death, and gang robbery with murder.

I had the serial killer example I mentioned earlier in mind when I wrote the following section.

I think life is sacred and precious. We only get one chance at it. A fundamental precondition to society is that we do not intentionally harm each other, even if we want to. We can think it all we like; however, we are safe as long as we don't act on it, or have others act on it. We are under a duty to not harm each other. So, any member of the community who disagrees with this and acts on this impulse to the physical detriment or death of someone else, while taking pleasure in it, must be excised from the community.

I am mindful of the possibility of error, of the conviction of an innocent person. I am also aware that a person can make such a grave and serious error out of passion, recklessness, or thoughtlessness, and still bear hope of reform.

Therefore, the element of repetition or the possibility of it by the offender is important. Killing one person once can be a mistake but not several—one after the other, over time. The lack of redeemability in the offender is crucial. If they toy with their kill or have some ritual to their killing then they are likely to repeat it.

However, if there is a possibility of reform, even an ambiguous one, it should be explored before considering the death sentence. Or, if there is potential for them to be useful for the benefit of humankind, for example, for medical purposes, they should be executed after any benefit or advantage that can be wrung out of them.

I do not approve of the State utilizing precious resources to keep such offenders alive. It should not have to spend money on maintaining someone who is a danger to society and has no hope for reform.

Keeping them alive, simply as a demonstration of our humanitarian values, ignores the financial commitment to such an empty gesture, as well as the incongruity and irony of keeping alive someone who delights in the harming and destruction of others. The State's record of its policies and initiatives should be considered, instead of its attitude to one issue before coming to judgment about its values.

I prefer asking, *What do you think of the death penalty?*

This question allows for nuance to arise in one's view about the issue. It avoids pushing one into a corner and having to explain our way out of it.

How Can You Defend a Criminal, Ah?

The archetypical question posed to me by laypersons , once they discover my dilettante with criminal law, are:

How cans you defending criminal when chew know he do it already? Aren't chew helping him gets away with its? Don't chew feel bad or guilty for helping him escapes the law, you pompous sounding wanker?

Allow me to address these questions, in as simple terms as possible, once and for all—if not for others, then for myself, at least.

To understand a criminal lawyer's ethical and moral outlook in defending any person accused of a crime, two preliminaries must be clarified, explained, and understood.

Accused is not the same as criminal

The first thing that requires clarification is the terminology. Descriptions are important and necessary because they categorize a person's relation to society. To be categorized wrongly is potentially defamatory, as I shall demonstrate shortly.

A person charged with a crime is not a 'criminal' because they have not been convicted of their crime. To charge someone is to merely 'accuse' them of something. At that stage, no evidence has been found to prove their crime. So, someone who has been charged with a crime should properly be referred to as 'an accused'.

Only after the court convicts an accused person can they be referred to as 'a convict' or a 'criminal'. One of the cardinal principles of criminal law is that a person is innocent until proven guilty beyond reasonable doubt.

Whoever refers to an accused as a 'convict' or a 'criminal' is vulnerable to liability in defamation, if the accused is acquitted at the end of the trial. This is because that description of them is legally wrong and defamatory.

The Rule of Law

The second aspect is the rule of law. I am sketching this part.

In the past, law enforcement was the sole prerogative of a ruler (back then, it was the king or queen) simply because the law was whatever the ruler had prescribed. This is known as the rule of whim. Modern constitutional developments have diluted and divided the ruler's power into the rule of law, which comprises three branches of government.

These are the legislature (power to make law), the executive (power to execute the law) and the judiciary (power to regulate and interpret the law to ensure that the actions of legislature and executive are constitutional). These branches of government are supposed to act as checks and balances against each other.

If the legislature enacts a law that infringes upon the Federal Constitution, the judiciary can strike it down. If the executive does something *ultra vires* (exceeding) the law, the judiciary can declare that action void. If the judges are corrupt, the executive can charge and prosecute them. If the judiciary makes a series of poor decisions in an area of law, the legislature can enact a law to overrule them. This power of a ruler was diluted and divided in order to avoid tyranny in the form of authoritarianism or totalitarianism.

Rule of Law, Not Rule of Whim

The rule of law demands that the legal process be fair, equal, accountable, and transparent in contrast to the rule of whim, where whatever the ruler says is the final word. How that demand translates at a criminal trial level is as follows.

Firstly, an impartial and honest judge, with or without a jury, hears all the evidence before guilt is decided upon. Secondly, the prosecution must bring evidence to prove the crime against an accused. Thirdly, the accused has the right to get sufficient time to prepare their case, hear the evidence against them, challenge it (either factually or legally), and have someone familiar with the law defend them in front of an impartial judge.

All these fundamental attributes must exist in reality, before a fair trial can be said to have taken place. The trial will, inevitably, be unfair if any of these attributes do not exist.

A short demonstration should suffice. If the judge is biased and does not have to hear evidence from both sides before deciding, they can convict an accused after hearing only the prosecution's side. If the prosecution does not have to bring any evidence to secure a conviction, an accused can be immediately convicted without an opportunity to challenge its evidence. They will not know why the prosecution charged them for such a crime. This is illustrated eloquently in the most claustrophobic terms by Franz Kafka's famous novel *The Trial.*

If an accused is not given any right to prepare their case, challenge the evidence, or a competent counsel, they would be at a fatal disadvantage compared to the prosecution, which has the entire resources and machinery of the State to prosecute the accused. The playing field is not, and never is, equal.

So Why, Ah?

With terminology clarified and the context of our criminal trial understood, we are now in a better position to understand why lawyers defend or, more accurately, are duty-bound to defend any person accused of a crime, regardless of their thoughts or feelings and moral orientation.

The rule of law makes it the incumbent duty of a lawyer to defend any person accused of any crime, because in defending them, that lawyer also sustains the very system of a fair trial. That incumbent duty also lies with a judge, but it is expressed differently because of the nature of their task. The judge must ensure a fair trial and decide honestly.

Finally, the duty lies with the prosecutor to prosecute the accused fairly and truthfully. All three must be faithful to their duties simultaneously, if the trial is to remain fair.

If this occurs at every trial, then a fair trial system is maintained; if it is lacking then it will break down. You only need one unfair trial to potentially create a systemic breakdown of the entire system and process of a fair trial. You cannot say we have a system of fair trial. However, there are exceptions: For example, for cases of sodomy involving an opposition politician. You either have a system of fair trial or you do not. It is not a question of percentage.

When this is understood, it is more easily and clearly seen that defending an accused person is not simply about their innocence or guilt. It is actually about sustaining, maintaining, and defending a fair trial system. This is why, for a criminal lawyer, whether their client committed the crime or not, or how they feel about his innocence or guilt, is irrelevant in the larger scheme. It is also not their responsibility, which is limited to merely testing the relevance and truth of the prosecution's evidence and ensuring the judge is fair. The judge must decide the innocence or guilt of the accused.

That single act of defending in one case is merely part of the criminal lawyer's wider expression and their collective series of actions in the larger scheme of justice. With each case a lawyer defends, they reinforce that ideal system of a fair trial. If a lawyer does not take up a case simply because they think the accused is guilty, and many echo that sentiment, who will finally defend that system and idea of a fair trial when the judge and the prosecutor have betrayed their duties? Without a lawyer to test the prosecution's evidence, every charge against an accused would end with a conviction. This, as anybody can appreciate, is manifestly unfair.

A true criminal lawyer is, and should be, unconcerned about their thoughts or feelings about an accused. They should be heedless about the media, their friends, their family, and society's thoughts and feelings about the matter. A trial is not about what anybody thinks of it; it is really about the sustenance of the system of justice. This is why we are obliged to challenge and take up any reasonable objection against the charge, if the accused pleads not guilty. The act of challenging ensures the quality of prosecution. It ensures the prosecution's evidence is high, and meets the standard of proof, which is beyond a reasonable doubt.

Prosecutor, Judge, and Lawyer: Different Roles

Prosecutors and judges, who view defence lawyers as a nuisance or annoyance, in truth do not understand the criminal legal system, or even their respective roles within it. The lawyer is as necessary, if not more, than the prosecutors or judge, because they are theoretically the most independent.

A prosecutor is part of the executive, and the judge is part of the judiciary. From the perspective of international and administrative law, both form part of the government administration. Both the prosecutor and the judge are in very powerful positions, so both, according to Lord Acton[18], are as potentially vulnerable as they are powerful to institutional prejudice and corruption (in the broadest sense of the word: intellectual, financial, moral, etc.).

Finally, both the prosecutor and judge can be directed by the powerful, influential, and political elite to do their bidding, when they do not possess sufficient ethical courage and moral conviction to resist the wealth, convenience, and power that corruption brings.

The common lawyer, however, is not ordinarily close to a political power source. Their role as a lawyer is not dependent on powerful political forces or patronage. For this reason, I consider that a lawyer who betrays their duties, of acting without fear or favour in the interest of justice, actually commits a greater act of betrayal to the system of a fair trial and, consequently, justice. History has shown that whenever the system has been under attack, prosecutors are often the first to betray justice. The next in line are judges. Of course, noble ones fight the good fight, but they are the first to be sidelined or sacked and never thrive and assume influential positions.

---

[18] Lord Acton refers to John Emerich Edward-Dalberg-Acton. He was a nineteenth century English historian, politician, and man of letters. He is best known for his famous remark: 'Power tends to corrupt, and absolute power corrupts absolutely.'

It is the lowly lawyer who is the last defence of justice. They bear the heavy burden of being that final hope of keeping the ideal of a fair trial alive, whenever the institutions of justice collapse. It is the lawyer who must be the conscience of justice, for the judge is its fountain and prosecutor the enforcer. All three of them, collectively, represent different facets of justice.

This is why equity demands that those who come to the court do so with the cleanest possible hands, cleaner souls, and the clearest intentions—especially those tasked with creating, shaping, and dispensing justice. One hand may defend it, but all three are the prerequisite for proper dispensation. If any of them lack these vital attributes, they have no business in the courts of law, never mind the realm of justice.

A lawyer who turns to cowardice and complacency, and colludes with judges or prosecutors, betrays and thwarts not only justice, but also demeans their counterparts at law, while sacrificing the entire nation on the altar of self-interest and corruption.

When all this is understood, the earlier questions appear to miss the point. Those asking them appear to have a narrow conception and micro perspective of the purpose of a criminal trial. It is not simply a process the 'bad guys' go through before being sent to jail, which many laypersons may naturally misunderstand it to be. They tend to not appreciate the broadness of the legal system, or the larger principles of justice, in which a criminal trial operates—often failing to even understand the meaning of a trial in the larger scheme of things.

Defending the Criminal is Defending Justice

So, a lawyer defending an accused is not simply defending them, but also reinforcing the administration of justice.

Whenever somebody asks me how I feel about defending an accused I think is guilty, I tell them I am perfectly fine with it. This reply often draws funny looks and, no doubt, leads them to believe that I'm one of those lawyers who lies and cheats to make money off criminals.

Although, not many are patient enough to understand this. First, it is not my job to decide upon their guilt; that is for the courts to decide. Second, in carrying out my job and defending them, I am playing an important role in sustaining and preserving the administration of justice.

That is the least any lawyer, judge, or prosecutor should strive for.

My Criminal Practice

Even though I have conducted criminal cases for my entire career in practice—at twenty-plus years now—I am not known as a criminal litigator. I have tackled everything: from petty thefts to attempted murder in the subordinate courts, all the way up to the High Court for drug trafficking, kidnapping and murder, as well as criminal appeals and applications in the Court of Appeal and Federal Court.

Some are surprised to learn I also conduct criminal cases. I am generally known for my involvement in civil, corporate, constitutional, and administrative law disputes, something which the reported cases testify to—just like my dabbling in criminal cases.

But that is fine. Despite my aforementioned long experience in criminal practice, I have never really considered myself to be a criminal litigator or introduced myself as one. I consider myself a litigator with a passion for conducting criminal cases and a concern for the administration of the criminal justice system.

To me, a criminal litigator pursues criminal cases day in day out, relentlessly tackling one after the another—a police station or another, most days; theft in the morning, drug trafficking in the afternoon; sodomy tomorrow, robbery the day after, and two child molestations the week after—with pleas of guilt, bail, and remand applications running alongside every day.

And I don't have such a practice.

I don't let my passiveness with criminal cases get in the way of cultivating a criminal litigation gig. I have always had the good fortune of having a few criminal cases in hand at any point throughout my career. The best way to do that is to seek out those who are desperate for legal representation.

For that, I have to thank the Bar Council Legal Aid Clinic, Kuala Lumpur for being my main source of criminal cases early in my career. These days, most of my appointments are as a court-appointed counsel from the High Court, appellate courts, or from the National Legal Aid Foundation (known as *Yayasan Bantuan Guaman Kebangsaan* or YBGK).

That is not to say *all* my criminal cases have come from there.

Occasionally, I am pleasantly surprised to find myself retained for criminal matters. Such events are always to be grateful for, given their uncommonness. I am also pleased to have my efforts acknowledged with appropriate remuneration.

I have let many opportunities slip by. I aim to keep those I advise grounded and realistic about their options, avoiding speculative, stupid, or overly ambitious ideas. I emphasize that my role is to only defend them in court, and I don't have any jalan[19].

There were two spells in my career when I intensely conducted criminal cases.

The first was around 1999 to 2005, back when I was a young, motivated lawyer, hungry for experience and learning. I took on all kinds of cases, criminal and civil, at the KL LAC, with gusto to sandpaper polish my meagre abilities and soak up as much experience as possible. That period was foundational to my criminal, civil, and advocacy experience.

---

[19] No other ways or avenues.

The second was when I set up the firm, between 2016 and 2017. My colleagues and I did not have much paid work on our hands because we had few clients back then. Hence, I signed us up for a slew of criminal matters from the legal aid clinic, as well as the YBGK, to keep ourselves busy.

The area of criminal litigation is wide these days.

There is the blue-collar crime of theft, robbery, and grievously injuring someone. There is also the white-collar crime of securities offences, stock market manipulation, and money laundering. There are now specialist courts for each: anti-corruption, child-centric, and cybercrime, for example. There is a slew of statutory offences for doing or not doing something. New ways of cross-examination must be learned for child and security offence cases.

Most of my cases are the old-fashioned variety of blue-collar crime: someone trafficks drugs, someone hurts or kills another person, someone destroys somebody else's property, kidnaps, attempts murder, or cheats another out of money—that kind.

These days, criminal litigation makes up for a maximum of 3 per cent of my work. I find it amusing when applicants, interns, and lawyers express interest to work with me because of their interest in criminal legal practice. I barely have more than a handful at any given point.

Regarding fee contributions for the firm, criminal legal practice has been almost non-existent, compared to my civil and even Syariah work. The court counsel fees are a token we are obligated to pay. The YBGK fees, however, are of the at-least-we-get-paid-something rate! At times, I take up these cases at a cost to myself. But then, before YBGK, back at the

KL LAC, we are not remunerated, except for a transport claim of fifty ringgit.

So, why should one practice criminal law, if there is no money in it and having to do it at one's own expense?

I can understand it may sound odd to some, but I nonetheless pursue them because of the genuine enjoyment I derive. I get restless if I don't get my fix for criminal cases through an appeal or a trial, with its respective pleasures and challenges. Essentially, it's the same skillset as my advocacy for civil litigation, just tweaked for the criminal setting.

I like the law involved with criminal litigation, for I get to unearth facts from the evidence like an archaeologist, also making sense of the events like a historian. I even savour cross-examining cops for personal pleasure. Crafting submissions for criminal cases is also something I tend to enjoy for the pleasant break it offers from civil practice, which tends to teem with documents.

Criminal litigation also challenges my analytical, imaginative, and advocacy abilities. It is about finding the gaps in the prosecution's case and recognizing an emerging gap or an unexpected weakness as it unravels. We have to think quickly and make several judgement calls on the fly, without the security of a pile of affidavits or bundles of documents to refer to, as we would in civil litigation cases.

All this keeps me sharp and allows my outlook to diversify. My criminal practice also allows me to meet people I would otherwise never know about and lets me learn about them. Pretty early on, I appreciated how fortunate I had been. I get to roam about a different area of law, away from my civil, paper-heavy matters. I have acquired a criminal litigation dimension, which adds to my overall legal sensibility and consideration of cases. Plus, there are interesting stories to tell others!

In taking up the mantle of defence, I contribute to the administration of the criminal justice system, which cannot function with just a judge and prosecutor alone—that would be tyrannical. The system requires all three to be in place to work as it should. Each one of them is necessary for the system to be whole, as justice is an emergent phenomenon from those three elements.

The prosecutor weaves a narrative and produces evidence for why a person should be convicted of a crime. The defence subjects the prosecution's narrative to intense scrutiny and tests them against predictable legal standards. The court considers whether to accept the prosecution's case on its own, and whether the defence raises a reasonable doubt about the charge against them.

All three need to be people of independence, integrity, industry, interest, and intelligence. Perhaps that is too much to ask for, but if any of the three lack these qualities, the administration of the criminal justice system will corrupt, as any system would.

As a lawyer, I do my part for the administration by defending a person accused of a crime. Anyone accused of an offence is entitled to a defence. Doing my part means, as best as I can, challenging the prosecution's evidence, putting my client's defence (assuming there is one) and articulating their arguments at trial or an appeal as effectively as possible, whilst expressing those aforementioned qualities.

That is easier said than done, especially when the stakes are high, cynicism is wide and deep, and there is an imbalance of power. With due process statutorily tilted against an accused and the machinery of the state working against them, each human being on trial is reduced to a mere statistic for someone else's pursuit of achievements.

These are the things we have to endure if we want to practice criminal law, which will not get in the way of the pleasure of the practice.

But only if we do not pay too much attention to it.

A GENERALLY CIVIL PRACTICE

A Resolutely Major Generalist

Sometime last year, a lawyer friend, whom I've known for some time, called me. After exchanging pleasantries, he told me he needed help with a matter.

'I thought of bringing you in. But then, I realized that I didn't know your practice area. Sorry for not being aware, despite knowing you for so many years.'

'Aiyah, no worries, lah. My practice area . . . How about this? Why don't you tell me what help you need, and I'll tell you whether I can help you. If I can't, I can recommend and refer you someone else.'

'Ha? So mysterious! Tell, lah!'

When pressed about my specialization, I respond by saying I'm a generalist. If I had to describe my law practice, it would be a full-caps generalist in the total sense.

While I am happy to spend time in an area of law, I have difficulty devoting an entire career to it. If I repeatedly confront the same specific fact, patterns, and laws, without meaningful and enough variation, practice becomes routine, boring, and tedious. For me, that ends with cynical despair.

It is not that I don't want to devote my career to an area of law.

I just can't—I am not made for it; it is against my grain.

I can't get enough spice from the variety that law offers.

I see a constellation of legal areas for my curiosity to slake itself and thrive on the contrast and colours that come from regular servings of a diversity of cases. I get excited when I am greeted by the fresh, dew-tinged vistas each time I enter a new area of law. I love the disorienting sense of discovery, the humbling awareness of how little I know and the pleasure of accumulating and integrating new learning.

The freshness from discovery, re-discovery, learning, and application keeps me curious and motivated. The complexity and effort that go into dealing with several areas of law at once keeps me challenged. My chase for such highs drives me out of my comfort zone into unfamiliar ones.

That drive expands my zone of competency and comfort.

A broad and moderately deep experience across several practice areas suffices. I don't, can't, and won't know all of them. However, the broader my experience and awareness, the more helpful I can be to a situation or someone. Being able to advise or represent holistically and comprehensively brings me deep personal satisfaction: I feel like a positive addition to society, even as I am advising someone on a charge of murder.

I want to help the many, instead of the few. The former involves attending to the usual areas of dispute, which can often be broad, such as the law on contract, tort, corporate, crime, family, etc. For it's as vast as it is varied, I am fascinated, invigorated, and anti-fragile. Helping the few involves dealing with matters that are niche or uncommon.

Because I had resisted specializing, for some time, I felt something was wrong with me. These days, I no longer feel the need to apologize for it. I accept that a general practice suits my character, abilities, and inclination. To my mind, there is nothing wrong with that.

In terms of law, I can advise and conduct. For example, tortious claims, contractual disputes, corporate disputes, administrative law challenges, constitutional law challenges, industrial claims, criminal cases, family claims for non-Muslims or Muslims, probate and administration, estate disputes, preparing contracts, trust deeds and legal instrument, notarization of documents and affirmation of sworn statements.

I consider myself and my colleagues sufficiently competent and experienced to represent, attend to, and advise others about their legal affairs and deliver a talk or two. We are trustworthy, competent, and dogged enough to conduct whatever matters to ensure our client's interests are privileged, protected, and advanced.

I am going to stop. I sound like a bloody ad.

Despite my seeming breadth of practice, I still feel what I know is merely a peasant's backyard vegetable patch in this vast plain of law. The Everest of what I don't know and perhaps will never know dominates the horizon of my knowledge, and I don't know what lies behind that Everest either.

I think being a generalist has many advantages. I will discuss a few for flavour.

I preface the discussion by clarifying: I do not endorse that being a specialist is inferior to, or lesser than, being a generalist. Both serve their respective purposes at the appropriate moments and have their inherent limitations and advantages. One is not better than the other.

Now, about those advantages.

Firstly, from a personal perspective, there is more to be interested in, curious about, and fascinated with regarding the law and legal practice. I am naturally inclined towards *generalism* because the kaleidoscope of the fascination it offers me. It's like sailing the seas, instead of lapping the lake. There's always something new to learn or existing to update. There are more legal adventures and new experiences to endure and enjoy in a broader arena. I do not lack fresh legal vistas. Boredom is non-existent.

Secondly, generalists are more sensitive to the array of potential legal issues in a given situation. For example, if a matter spans corporate, criminal, tort, Syariah, and administrative law, a generalist experienced in those areas will likely be sensitive to such issues and can advise and represent accordingly. A generalist is in a position to appreciate better the legal implications across various legal practice areas and factual scenarios. That appreciation enables consideration and formulation of a single, unifying, consistent, and cohesive strategy across the various areas.

Thirdly, practising in various areas has a compounding effect on our insights and skill set, which makes 2 + 2 = 5.5. Competency across various practice areas enables insights into those legal areas, particularly when intersecting. We can compare and contrast one practice area with another. Knowledge in one area informs the knowledge of other. Skills and strategies honed in one area benefit others too.

An example of this is advocacy. Usually, I have a clutch of criminal cases running alongside my regular practice. This hones my ability to think on my feet, sharpens my cross-examination, and broadens my imagination. Compared to my civil cases, particularly the document-heavy ones, I have to be sharper and quicker to react in my cross-examination in criminal cases.

In civil cases, everything is bestowed upfront: the claim, its basis, and the defence. If an application is involved, affidavits and written arguments are exchanged. If it's a trial, paginated document bundles with printed witness statements waiting to be affirmed are served in advance. There is much documentary orchestration and oral evidence choreography involved in civil proceedings.

It is less so for criminal cases, wherein we are given some documents the prosecution intends to adduce at trial. We don't always know who the witnesses will be, and we do not get witness statements before trial, which creates significant uncertainty about the best way to approach a defence. That, in turn, creates tremendous pressure to make a great deal of critical, spur-of-the-moment judgment calls throughout the trial and during arguments.

What I gain from one practice area can benefit my other areas.

Fourthly, inherent resilience and range develop from practising in various areas. The latter allows me opportunities to lean on or develop other practice areas when work in our regular practice areas slows down or decreases. Resilience, on the other hand, enables the diversification of risk.

Many practice areas have to be extinct before my legal practice is affected. Range enables opportunities for resilience, be it intellectual and financial. It is also a prerequisite for sustainability, something that I am looking to achieve.

Fifthly, being a generalist allows us to attend to various legal problems: from the common, to the contentious, to the unprecedented. We can provide legal services to a greater section of society, to people, natural or artificial, or a society of them. I think this point is the most obvious.

There are, of course, downsides to being a generalist. It's not all Sundays and sunshine.

Firstly, generalists do not usually dominate a particular practice area. They do not because they cannot. The multifaceted nature of this practice inhibits the establishment of a reputation for expertise or dominance in a particular area.

Secondly, generalists come off as vague and uncertain about what they do, which makes explaining to it others difficult. I recognize how ironic this is, given that law is reputedly all about black-and-white certainty. Generalists are, hence, more challenging to market and they have many competitors. Their practice is as ambiguous as it is nebulous— they don't have a niche.

I know everyone tells us to specialize. It is lucrative, niche, easy to dominate, and easier to market. Specializing is the way to go is something I read and hear all the time. It's standard, cliched advice.

But it's not for everyone: I'm one of them. As a generalist, I have difficulty claiming to be a specialist or an expert in any area.

Thirdly, and quite naturally, generalists will not know a practice area as deeply and completely as someone who has dwelled in a specific practice area for a long time. They will likely lack the nuance, deeper insights, and unique knowledge derived from a specialist practice. This makes generalists susceptible to the Dunning-Krueger effect, which involves overestimating our knowledge of an area we are ignorant about.

If I am to be a specialist in something, I choose to specialize in technique, not subject matter. My abilities enable me to advise and represent clients across various practice areas.

My focus is on the basics. I seek ways and opportunities to refine my reading, writing, thinking, speaking, and empathetic skills, as keeping them at a reasonably high operating level allows me to maintain range. Moreover, getting acquainted with a new area of law or practice is disorienting and difficult: I used to fret at how long it took to acquaint myself with a new legal area. Now, I don't worry. If I stay with it long enough, keep doing it over and over, and give it time, I am confident of gaining competency in that area. After that, it is simply a matter of interest and opportunity. The more I experience, the more I learn.

Another reason I can practice in a variety of areas is that we do not need to spend a great deal of time in a specific practice area to acquaint ourselves with it. But we have to be focused, patient, and diligent.

The Pareto principle states that 20 per cent of the causes are responsible for 80 per cent of the effects.

Before I proceed, please note that though I seem to use precise percentages, they are metaphors. The numbers indicate the emotional weight I allocate to it.

I don't know whether the Pareto principle applies to knowledge and experience in a legal area, but my belief is it does, though I have no studies, research, or proof to substantiate this claim, just my sense from experience.

The balance is closer to 30 to 35 per cent, which is, if we know the core 35 per cent, we can manage 70 to 75 per cent of the cases. Once we grasp the core 35 per cent, it lays the foundation to deal with most cases. The other 25 to 30 per cent we cannot deal with, go to the specialists, who will know it, because they are likely to have spent almost their entire career, or at least 85 to 100 per cent of it, in that practice area.

For example, consider criminal cases. If you are familiar with the foundational 35 per cent of criminal procedure and law, you can handle 70 per cent of the cases. By grasping the criminal trial process—such as where the burden of proof lies, what the standard of proof is, what is the burden on the defence, and principles of relevancy and evidentiary integrity—you will be equipped to challenge the material evidence and put forth the defence during the prosecution's case.

I know this because I knew a little less than the core 35 per cent when I took on my first criminal case in the Kuala Lumpur juvenile court and won.

It is similar with other areas of practice too.

We don't have to immerse ourselves forever to be good enough to practice it, and we don't need to know it all at once either. It is favourable if we are able to; if not, we can get there with persistent study. We can accumulate, assimilate, and integrate our knowledge when we encounter it more or less regularly.

With many of these new areas, get to the core 35 per cent. Spend time finding out what that core 35 per cent is or work it out. You can find the core from the statute, essential textbooks, practitioner's texts, academic commentaries, leading cases, and those practising in that area. Once you master the core, proceed further. Rinse and repeat in the following practice area. You will be surprised by how much you pick up after over twenty years of active and curiosity-driven legal practice, picking up the core 35 per cent here and there.

So, what really is a general practice, like mine?

It is a blast. I am pleased and privileged by the variety of work I get. I am particularly grateful to those who trust my colleagues and me to advise them and conduct their cases. It is rarely dull, though sometimes, it is complex, tedious, challenging, miserable, nerve-wracking, frustrating, annoying, or depressing.

But it is never boring. Some days, it's the best damn job in the world and immensely satisfying.

There have been days when I conducted a criminal trial in the morning, popped by the office to check on a conveyancing matter over lunch, and then was off to the civil court for a breach of contract trial.

There have also been days when I conducted a Federal Court hearing in the morning and then continued with a part-heard case in the Magistrates' Court in the afternoon.

There have been days when I conduct a Syariah court trial in the morning, and then an online hearing in the Court of Appeal in the afternoon.

There are days when I work on a divorce settlement agreement in the morning and share sale agreement in the afternoon.

There are also weeks when I am working on a heavy legal opinion and have meetings without any court to attend.

That is a taste of what my day could look like. Of course, there is more to it and many more possible permutations. The point really is the diversity of work and, therefore, experiences.

Not all generalists are the same or can be compared. Each has a unique configuration of skill sets, attitudes, and experiences, with each configuration having its own advantages, expertise, and limitations.

I don't think we can meaningfully convince anyone to be a generalist any more than we can be convinced to be a specialist. It is in our bones: We are either inclined or not. We can work against our nature, of course, but we would be worse off and miserable about it.

The point is not whether we are generalists or specialists, but do we practice in a manner consistent with our nature, inclination, and attitude? If we do so, we avoid violating ourselves and can derive the most significant return of pleasure, fun, and resonance from our work and practice.

And that should be the goal for each lawyer, generalist, or specialist.

‘How Do You Get Work?’

One of my younger colleagues asked me this question the other day.

‘That is a good question,’ I admitted.

‘Thank you, Sir,’ he said.

‘I reply *good question* to questions I don’t know have the answers for.’

‘Really, Sir? Or are you being humble about it?’

‘I am not. Quite honestly, I don’t know how we get work, given I don’t market the firm. I neither indulge in social media marketing, nor cold calling people. I also don’t tout and couldn’t be arsed to get up early and go to business groups. Neither do I go around telling people we’re the best, greatest, latest, etc., and all other marketing superlatives. I don’t hang around people or companies in the hope work falls into my lap or try to get on every bank or company panel.’

‘I have difficulty doing that too,’ he said.

‘And if I am honest about it, I don’t like doing these things and don’t want to do them. My thought process is: I am a lawyer, not a marketeer. I am in the business of selling and evaluating arguments, not promoting myself or the firm. Of course, they will say marketing is now part of a lawyer’s skill. I disagree with that.’

‘I feel like many lawyers focus more on the business of law instead of the law,’ he added.

'Exactly. For myself, I want to do good, meaningful work for clients who appreciate us. And do it with people I like for an appropriate fee. It's that simple. If I can do that without marketing, so much the better. We don't need a lot of work; we need enough work.'

'How do we become known if we just concentrate on the work?'

'Let the experience and the quality of our work be our selling point. I prefer for us to devote the time, effort, and money we would have spent on marketing to the quality and experience of our legal service. I know I sound ancient, but personally, I see marketing and promotion as a distraction to the quality and focus of our work as lawyers. I want to see my lawyers cutting their teeth on cases instead of ornamenting their social media.

'So, even though I don't know the answer to your question, it raises a good point about our legal education. Although we are taught to do the work, we are never taught how to get the work. When I was younger, I thought that was a flaw of our legal education. But now that I am a little older and run my own firm, I realize now it wasn't a flaw, but a feature.'

'Why is that?'

'University could never teach us how to get work because university is academia; it's theory, not practice. Be careful about listening to a legal academic about how to get legal work. It is beyond their competency. Getting work is what we can only learn from the university of life. At the end of the day, it's about people and situations in action, not in books. Getting work is what you have to learn through observation, experience, and experiment, not some seven-step programme.'

'How do we get the work we do then?'

'I don't know, but my sense of it is that up to 60 per cent of it comes from peer referrals. Yes, most of our referrals come from lawyers, not the public. The rest, I'd guess, come from our current clients and friends and family who recommend us, the firm's reputation, and people who have somehow heard of us. As to how we get the work we do, I think it is similar to what a senior lawyer told me many years ago when I was a young lawyer and had the pleasure of sitting at the same table at dinner with him.'

'Is he still around?'

'Oh, yes. If you frequent the Palace of Justice in Putrajaya often enough, you will see him. Every time I have a case, I see him attending to a few. I would see him run from one appellate court to another for his appeals. That's how busy he was. Anyway, I heard how he ran a thriving counsel practice and wanted to learn how he established it. Since he was at the table, after some small talk, I could not resist asking, "Dato, how does one cultivate a counsel practice like yours? The reply came back swiftly.

"Do your best for every case that you appear for. Pour yourself into it. Don't take shortcuts with your work. The client will know. The court will know. And above all, you will know. Give it your best. The challenge is to make sure you do this for every case, no matter how big or how small. Many of the clients I came to have were those impressed with my performance in court. Even though I was against them in one case, they called me to act for them in the next. So, always, do your best in whatever work you do. People will hear, they will tell others, and then somehow you find yourself with more work.

'I'd adapt that answer to your question and add: Give each case and client the time, care, and attention that it needs or they need. Don't rush through it. Don't try to get away with the work. Listen patiently. Address the real concern the client is having and help them with it. When we can genuinely help others with their legal problems, they are likelier to recommend to others. That goes for referrals from the public, private and professional.'

'So, to get work, we should just focus on doing our best for it. That will eventually bring us more work?'

'Something like that.'

Working with Juniors and Myself

As a senior lawyer, I almost always work with a junior or two on matters. By junior, I mean a fresh or less experienced lawyer or a pupil, who would do the getting up for the case, which is preparing it for a hearing or trial. However, it is not a phrase often used these days.

In *getting up* a case, the junior is tasked with preparing the first draft of whatever we are working on. It can be an opinion, contract, application, or trial—basically, any piece of work. Before beginning, we discuss the case, the approach and direction, our intention to tackle the expected challenges, and whether they require clarifications and deadlines. I often tell my juniors to work it into the draft for discussion later, if they have a bright idea. Then, I leave them to it and see what comes back.

This is how it was with my boss, back when I started. Except, he just briefed me about the case and told me what he wanted done and when. The rest was for me to figure out.

For a fresh lawyer or pupil, the first draft is often the most difficult to write and, naturally, the easiest to make mistakes in, therefore, making it a fertile field for learning. After discussing the corrections and improvements in the first draft, I allow them to revise it. When they return the second draft, we discuss it. If it's still not close to what I want, we continue to discuss and revise it until I find it acceptable.

We learn best from our mistakes, which is why I deliberately create an environment that gives them the opportunity to make mistakes. So, when I do point it out, explain, and correct it—instead of scolding, belittling, or shouting at them—the lesson is clear, direct, and vivid to them. Or so I hope.

They learn by doing, not by simply being told or scolded. Belittling and shouting erect needless barriers to learning, wantonly damaging their nascent sense of confidence. And those who scold don't realize how mean, disrespectful, and egoistical they appear. This is not to say it is *never* warranted—it is; it's just not as often as we think.

Without aggression, the lesson I want to impart is clearer, and uncluttered with negative vibes. I intend them to go through the process of experiencing their mistake, the correction, and, most importantly, work out for themselves to avoid their mistakes. I give them a free hand with the drafts because I want them to develop their own style and not be constrained by mine. Although, if they do adopt it, that's fine. But I am nevertheless curious to see what theirs looks like.

So, there is often a certain amount of to-and-fro on the drafts. Even though it is my preferred teaching and working method, it can be painful if my junior is either mediocre, uninterested, or incapable of improvement. If they don't get meaningfully closer to my expectation by the third draft, and if I am unable to see any prospect of improvement, I let someone else have a go at it. But that is only if we have the time; if we don't, I complete it without them.

This method, however, would be pleasurable if I worked with a legal savant, whose drafts are often close to my expectations, if not entirely. There are moments when they exceed it, often allowing me to learn from them. Working on the drafts with them is less of a chore and more of an adventure in an intellectual cavern.

I *almost always* work with a junior, but not when a piece of work has great urgency, or is too difficult for them. In such a case, either a senior colleague handles it, or I do so myself, as there is no time for to-and-fro.

But sometimes, I do not want to work with anyone because I have a strong desire to do it all myself. I want to be the junior labouring at work, instead of supervising it. I want to come up with the drafts, do the research, prepare the application, write up the letters, craft the submission, draft a contract or opinion, and essentially take on all the bits of work that go towards the finished product.

But then, who checks my work? That would also be me. I often leave my drafts fallow, only to return to them after a while. No matter how short the time frame is, I must do this ritual: a few hours, if the time is short; a few days if otherwise. Leaving it alone lets me take that mental break to consider it afresh, thus allowing new ideas and insights to present themselves. It also helps me shift from a 'junior mindset' to a 'senior mindset' and approach it accordingly. Somehow, I am able to look over my draft, just as I would for a stranger. It is important for me to consider the drafts critically instead of defensively.

Only once that is done do I circulate my final draft to my colleagues for their feedback. I ask them to check it for errors, readability, sense, and persuasiveness. This isn't done every time, although, if I think it is important enough or am feeling unsure about it, I circulate it.

This desire to do it all by myself runs its course once the work is submitted, after which, I feel a great sense of personal satisfaction and accomplishment—as if my skills have been sharpened.

I enjoy assuming the junior role to not forget what it was like to be one. Moreover, in doing so, I can better empathize with the young lawyers and pupils I work with.

Just because I am a senior, doesn't mean I have to always feel, think, or pretend to be one.

A Pupil's Remuneration

Mathew Thomas Philip, a senior lawyer, recently made an interesting suggestion about the pupils' remuneration. He proposed to replace their allowances with a pupil loan, which allows for comfortable repayment terms. It is intended to remunerate the supervising lawyer for coaching of the pupil. Mathew reasons that since the pupillage period is an extension of their legal education after university, and because the pupils have already paid for their undergraduate and legal entrance exams, it follows that they should pay their masters or the firm for their continued tutelage.

I have read and heard much of the disagreement with Mathew's proposal. While I have no issues with the idea, I am disappointed with the vitriol it has received. I think it is uncalled for, especially when it comes from lawyers and soon-to-be lawyers. The man has put out an idea: We either agree or disagree with it, and provide our reasons for deciding, but that should be the end. This is how I imagine civil discourse to be, and how lawyers should engage. There is no need to disfigure the proposal and malign the man. To do otherwise is a disservice to our profession.

Mathew's proposal is not new: it is merely an old one with a twist. This was the position a long time ago, when pupils paid their masters for the privilege of an apprenticeship. According to Merriam-Webster Online, an apprentice is someone who is 'learning by practical experience under skilled workers a trade, art or calling'. The pupils, back then, did not pay their masters to be taught, but rather, for the opportunity to be present and to observe them practice their craft. A master is not in the business of teaching but of attending to their clients. The pupil's presence is, in truth, more often a hindrance than help. Of course, exceptions exist, but this is the general norm.

I once asked my father why he did not pass his work to the pupils. He replied that he didn't want to go back and forth on a simple draft for a week. 'I have no patience for that anymore,' he had said. 'If I can get it done in fifteen minutes and finish it, it is better. This way, I can get on with other things.'

I can attest to that sentiment, for it is tempting to take that route. What may take a pupil a week's time to finish to an acceptable standard can be tackled by an experienced and learned lawyer in half or three-fourth of a day. This, while assuming the pupil's abilities and qualities are useful.

Generally, there is a deep and wide gulf in experience and knowledge between a senior lawyer and a pupil or young lawyer. There will be newcomers, just as there will be incumbents, and hence, that gulf of expertise between the two is inevitable because we have no choice over the timing of our births. This is, therefore, the natural state of things in any profession or merit-based environment.

Mathew's twist on the old ways was the addition that pupils would not seek financing. Instead, they would be given a loan on generous terms, and thus, would be able to demand more training and education from the master. I am not with Mathew on this for a fundamental reason: My starting point is that pupillage is a privilege, not a right. There is no legal obligation for a senior lawyer to take on a pupil.

I disagree with the notion that pupillage is simply an extension of a pupil's formal legal education, and, therefore no different from university or Bar school. For me, when a person is ready for pupillage, they should be competent at self-instruction, that is, familiar with learning things for themselves. The precedent should be that I, as a supervisor, shouldn't be teaching a pupil how to learn things but point out what they should learn. Pupillage is an apprenticeship and, hence, an opportunity to apply theory to real-life situations, where pupils learn from the work given and the experience of doing it. A law firm isn't a teaching facility.

After all, I am not in the endeavour of educating; I run a legal business. Legal education does not contribute to the bottom line or even to the foreseeable future. Taking a pupil is also a voluntary gesture: They are a cost and not even an investment. Often, those who trouble themselves to educate their pupils think they must ensure the coming generation is better than ours to maintain the standards, if not improve, at the inevitable changing of the guard.

But, fairly, not everyone is like that. We cannot blame others for it or call them selfish—it is just how some lawyers want it to be, which they are entitled to. I can empathize with it: It's a far simpler existence; there is nobody else to worry about and pay for, and one doesn't have to put up with other people's shoddy work. Although it's a shame their 'craft' will not survive them, but it should not be held against them. It is their choice.

So, to recapitulate it, I think about pupils' remuneration with the following elements in mind, discussed above:

Firstly, pupillage is a privilege; secondly, it is an apprenticeship; thirdly, and generally, pupils come without the experience, skill set, or knowledge to fully assist in a matter and often assist on the periphery while they learn on the fly. Finally, it is a privileged apprenticeship, which means, there is no right to it. If there is no right to it, there is even less leeway to make demands about the remuneration.

If pupils insist on a particular pay, a particular sort of work, a particular sort of set up then there will be progressively fewer senior lawyers willing to take them on. I don't dub it a threat. None of us could be bothered to gang up together. I am merely asserting that imposing more onerous requirements to take a pupil on will likely serve as a disincentive for senior lawyers, and the economics of it won't make sense.

So, these demands about remuneration, contracts, etc., are, with respect, misplaced. They misunderstand the relationship between the master and the pupil, and are caught up more with short-term self-interests. Whether pupils should be paid or not is a debate long past. They should be paid, and to have them pay us for an apprenticeship in this day and age is inappropriate.

Pupils need to keep this in perspective when they demand remuneration: They do not contribute to the firm in terms of finding clients, closing out appointments, doing important work, conducting trials or hearings by themselves, issuing invoices, negotiating fees, recovering unpaid fees, and making sure the staff are paid on time, for example. Of course, a pupil taking up firm work should be remunerated for it, but they should not overestimate their contribution, for their presence is not critical to the organization's existence. It will go on with or without them because law firms are not set up to cater to pupillage but the clients' legal needs.

However, as pupils are under their charge, masters are ethically and morally obligated to provide a reasonable allowance for them as per the firm's economy and not use them primarily for non-legal or menial work. Pupils should be paid on time, their claims made quickly, and they should be given appropriate work. If possible, their attendance for Bar-organized courses should either be subsidized or paid for, which is often affordable. Whether that allowance should cover a pupil's living expenses is for the firm to decide.

If pupils don't agree with the remuneration terms, they should either leave or not sign up. But if they do end up staying, don't whine after that. It's unprofessional. And nobody is forcing you to do it. If you are unhappy, quit. Keep looking for a pupillage position that fits you and your expectations, and all the best with that.

To me, pupils who are more concerned about their allowance than the experience have their priorities in the wrong place and possess a short-term outlook. While they don't like it when senior lawyers say this, it is likely they will share the same sentiment when they reach our level of experience, which is fifteen years and above.

For me, this is the litmus test. If you get to a pupil with a legendary senior lawyer but you have to do so for free, are you going to accept or decline it? If you decline it for some inconvenience, it is best to leave the practice immediately, because it is not meant for you. A pupillage is not for the pupil to earn a living—they are off in nine months unless retained—but a privileged opportunity to learn earning a living from a practitioner of the craft. That's what being a lawyer is, a craft, and that's what a pupil or young lawyer is, an apprentice.

Pupils should be concerned about the person they are going to be working with or under, the type of work they will be exposed to or required to do, how independently they are expected to work, what they are allowed to do in relation to work, the firm's policy on legal aid, and so forth. They should also thoroughly research their intended firm or master.

All of these matters will set up a pupil for the long-term, not the allowance.

To me, those who choose their pupillage primarily based on allowance are unaware of their own expectations from the experience. Hence, they pivot to money by default because of the safety if offers. Statements like, 'Even if I didn't enjoy the experience, at least I was well remunerated,' fool us into thinking that it is about the money. A pupil who talks more about remuneration than the law is going to be unhappy later on because they are unlikely to speak about either at some point.

One should spend the early part of their years focusing on building competency and cultivating reputation, not pay. The former will be paid to you handsomely in the future.

But if you think short-term, you will prioritize the pay to be as high a sum as you can get early on in your career. People who think short-term, won't last long-term.

A Master's Expectation

This intense discussion about pupil remuneration revealed an interesting dimension to the issue: A master's expectation of their pupil. The impression is that pupils are expected to be 'practice ready', that is, they should be able to draft letters, applications, and submissions competently; be familiar with going about court, dealing with clients, and generally have an understanding of conducting a case, etc. Inabilities or shortcomings, if any, tend to be blamed on their tertiary education—the universities.

Mohd Hazmi Mohd Rusli and Noor Dzuhaidah Osman, two academics, in a letter to the press, disagree that tertiary education is responsible for these supposed shortcomings. They wrote:

> Law faculties are not law firms and have limited means to sufficiently provide comprehensive legal training to them.
>
> It is to be remembered that law schools do not only produce legal practitioners, but also future academics, bankers, administrators, diplomats and the like.
>
> Law graduates could only experience hands-on legal training when they undergo pupillage or chambering at legal firms. If law graduates are expected to know everything and

> to be practice-ready from day one, what is then the purpose of the nine-month pupillage?[20]

In short, universities provide legal education, not legal training, which comes under the province of pupillage and, hence, law firms. This, to my mind, is fair.

I didn't get one whit of legal training when I was a university student. If a friend had not dragged me to a moot court once, I am certain I would have confused it with a moat! This was as close to legal training as I received. Even when we sat for our certificate of legal practice, or CLP[21], we received no legal training, just more 'legal education', which was essentially stuff we had to memorize and regurgitate.

We were not trained to draft claims or defences but only acquainted with their formats. There were no advocacy or client-handling classes either nor were we taught opinion writing or research skills. This starkly contrasted with those who had finished the Bar course and returned to Malaysia as barristers after being called to the Bar in England. They were also legally trained and tested to be practice-ready. If they complete their pupillage in England, pupils must earn their keep during the latter six months after their initial six months. However, there is no such burden on the Malaysian pupil.

At the very least, we possessed basic abilities, which included the knack to read critically, with discernment, and write and speak sensibly in order to discuss matters in a civil manner. These fundamental skills, along with a knowhow

---

[20] Mohd Hazmi Mohd Rusli & Noor Dzuhaidah Osman (2020) Letter: Law graduates unprepared for pupillage?, Malaysiakini. Available at: https://www.malaysiakini.com/letters/551798 (Accessed: 16 December 2024).

[21] In Malaysia, the CLP is the qualifying exam for us to be lawyers. The CLP examinations are conducted by the Legal Profession Qualifying Board (lpqb.org.my).

of researching legal issues and formulating them, would be grasped to some degree at the university. The rest we learned on the go.

Instead of courses, seminars, and webinars to learn from, we faced the judge's ire, scolding, and the embarrassment that followed—which often served as the impetus to learn fast. We were bloody but unbowed. Back then, this experience was expected to be endured by someone finding their place in the legal world.

Even though the availability of training and courses compared to today was negligible, it did not mean we were incompetent. It just meant taking a little longer to reach where we were supposed to because we had been learning from raw experiences. However, what we possessed back then was time. Masters, too, had more patience owing to the pace of practice, which was unlike today's. Sometimes, I wonder whether this swiftness contributes to the unreasonableness of expectations sought of the pupils.

The difference between then and now is that there was little to no expectation for a pupil to be practice-ready. If they possessed those skills to a high degree, nothing like it; it would make them exceptional. While we appreciate that exceptional cases are uncommon, we seem to place expectations reserved for the exceptional on the ordinary. This is where, I think, the unreasonable expectations of being 'practice ready' find their source.

Unreasonable expectations also provoke unreasonable demands, which explains the dissatisfaction and grievance on both sides of the equation.

We must acknowledge that if there is such an expectation from pupils to be practice-ready, it is unreasonable and unhealthy. I certainly didn't feel I was practice-ready even after completing pupillage, never mind at the very start.

How was I to, when I came straight from 'legal education'. During pupillage, my predominant concern was making sure I did not screw up whatever was handed to me, which I nonetheless did.

Right out of the door, I had made a mistake in my call papers[22], which was of a single alphabet and something I had to amend. I wrote ***saujana***[23] *muda undang-undang* instead of ***sarjana***[24] *muda undang-undang*[25]. From such a tiny but critical error, early in my pupillage, I learned how to draft an amendment application, the supporting affidavit, and prepare an amended form. I also familiarized myself with using the office typewriter. Most importantly, I learned what I had to do if there was a need to amend something in the future.

Mistakes are important junctures of learning. Being practice-ready implies not making mistakes anymore because, as lawyers, we can't afford to—despite our humble humanity involved. This perhaps accounts for the stress and anxiety now commonly associated with pupillage. My pupils routinely apologize for being unable to reach my expectations before they even proceed with the work. I find it puzzling and amusing.

What I tell them is more or less this:

'Look, I don't expect a perfect first draft. If you are able to manage that, great! But since you are just starting out, just do it how you think it should be done. I will tell you what you got right and what needs improvement. The ultimate point is to improve on it until it becomes acceptable to our standards. You only need to apologize if you didn't give me your best shot.'

---

[22] These are the court documents filed for my admission to the Bar as an advocate and solicitor.

[23] 'Wide' or 'far' in Malay.

[24] 'Scholar' in Malay.

[25] The Malay equivalent of Bachelor of Laws.

Masters and firms must dial down their expectations for pupils a few notches, and move away from the notion they should be practice-ready. While having standards is important to our profession, we must also recognize that each pupil's abilities need to be assessed individually. They will have different qualities, trajectories, arcs, and developmental momentums. However, this is hard to assess when pupils are taken in bulk. If we do not take the trouble to get a sense of where they stand, we may harm, stall, or misguide that development and fail to nurture their potential.

Masters today must take some responsibility and interest in their pupil's development. This means assigning them appropriate legal work, providing guidance when required, explaining what it means to be a lawyer, sending them to courses, and getting to know them as people. They should also have a visible presence in the pupil's experience. If they want to do more, that is even better. Without these elements, especially a strong rapport with their masters, pupillage can feel transactional, which make it easy for feelings of ill-treatment to stir.

We must acknowledge that not all masters are angels; some of them can be quite the devil. I have heard complaints, now and again, from pupils at other firms, about their mistreatment. I feel sorry for them. From what they tell me, some of the treatment goes beyond the rigours of merely intense work and spills into the realm of psychological and emotional abuse.

This must stop. Everyone has a role to play: Pupils need to report such misconduct; the Malaysian Bar must take such complaints seriously and prosecute them; and lawyers sitting over such complaints must call it as they see it, without shielding offending colleagues. If any party fails to carry out their responsibilities, it results in the failure of the process and, if it done repeatedly, failure of the system.

These days, few masters call me up to arrange their pupil's calls; more often, it is the pupils who approach me directly. I find it concerning, as I am a stickler about these things. This highlights the delinquency of some masters, as it is their responsibility to arrange for the pupil's mover. The reason for it is simple—pupils often lack the connections to approach senior lawyers themselves. An introduction by the masters is, therefore, important.

A master's expectations must be reasonable and aligned with the pupil's state of development and potential. They must be mindful of their obligations towards their pupils and trouble themselves to carry them out. This is the first step, I think, to untangle the twisted knots of unreasonable expectations and demands.

The second cut is for lawyers and pupils who clamour for employment contracts and wages for pupils to research pupillage history, the experiences and remuneration of pupils in other commonwealth jurisdictions, and the standards expected of those pupils when they commence their training as a vital starting point.

From there, I hope both sides can engage in a civil, mature, and informed position. Hopefully, it should be the final cut.

'You Can Scold Me, Sir'

Every now and then, a pupil or an intern will express their willingness to learn and emphasize that I scold them. 'Please feel free to scold me; I have no problems with it,' they say. 'You can even shout at me. If you do so, it would mean I deserve it.'

To scold is to speak angrily to somebody—say, a child—for doing something wrong. To shout, on the other hand, is to speak loudly or angrily to somebody.

There are variations to it, of course.

The funniest one emerged during a pupil interview I had conducted, where the candidate assured me she was willing to work hard. 'I have no problem with staying back after hours, Sir,' she said. 'Nor do I have issues with a higher workload. You can give me as much as you want. Feel free to even grind me.' Quickly, I hastened to correct her, suggesting that perhaps she meant to add 'with work' to her last sentence. I cautioned her to be more careful with her words in the future.

While I appreciate and feel grateful for the wide liberty granted to me by those who seek to learn from me, I find the offer equally tragic and amusing.

Amusing because their statement is an invitation for me to inflict verbal abuse upon them wantonly; however, at the same time, it is not my teaching approach. This is like handing me a chainsaw for something I am happy using feather dusters for. Thank you, but I'll stick to the feathers.

I prefer empathy, support, guidance, and reassurance over worship, scolding, guilt, and humiliation. The latter, even if takes more time, effort, and patience, helps build better resilience, meaningful confidence, and coping mechanisms in people in the long-term.

I don't engage in verbal abuse either. However, if someone believes that abuse is necessary for learning something during their internship or pupillage, they may be disappointed to find that there is a fee for that. Instruction is free; abuse however, is chargeable.

It is sad because the implicit assumption in such invitations is the idea that abuse is a required price for education. It represents that they are trapped within the limitations of their imagination.

It is tragic because the notion of 'abuse', intertwined with the idea of education, is surprisingly widespread. When I refer to 'abuse', I am talking about verbal and psychological mistreatment. But the greater tragedy, though, lies in the failure to understand what learning truly entails.

First and foremost, we do not need to learn exclusively from a person or an educational institution. We can learn from a bunch of sources—or none at all. We can learn from books, videos, incidents, courses, even insects or animals, and, most importantly, from our own experience. Learning occurs when we reflect and think deeper about what we already know or have experienced.

While learning from others can be beneficial, not everyone is worth learning from. A suitable mentor can accelerate one's professional and personal development, but it is crucial to know that not everyone knows how to facilitate learning. Just because someone excels in their field, doesn't mean they can teach as effectively. A well-reputed teacher or a mentor might not always be appropriate for us, and not everyone gratuitously wants the best for us.

Finding a suitable teacher is as challenging as finding a suitable life partner: They must be 'fit'. When teachers and students are suitable for each other, they connect not just in the dimension of legal practice but also psychologically, emotionally, intellectually, and in terms of attitude. There is a merging of minds, which revitalizes and reshapes both.

However, teachers do not necessarily have to be qualified, as long as they speak from genuine experience and insight. They need not even be necessarily older or more experienced than us, as I often learn from my children, younger colleagues, non-lawyers, etc. Though inconspicuous, there are lessons to be learned from them.

Secondly, learning does not only happen in a classroom, lab, university lecture, tutorial, courtroom, or some institutionalized formal space. It can happen anytime, and everywhere, even in in the most innocuous of places, where we least expect it. Those moments of epiphany or insight—when our accumulated, distilled thoughts burst into consciousness—often take place when we are doing something else.

We need to be observant and open. Stay humble curious, and don't expect and insist on a particular outcome. This allows the leeway for learning to take place.

Thirdly, learning is something only we can do for ourselves. While others can certainly help us, they cannot execute it for us. So, studying is a lot like sleeping, eating, peeing, and the like—only we can do it for ourselves.

We must strive to personally engage with the material or experience how to make sense of it. The latter part forms the core of our learning, where we are working things out for our own sake. In the same process, we come to understand our place and role in this bodily existence. This sense-making is what we must cultivate and refine, without letting someone else do it for us.

Fourthly, we must learn how to *learn* things better—for it is equally a discipline and a pleasure. Moreover, it is a learned ability, which comes naturally to some, and can be taught, refined, and improved in others.

Studying smarter does not simply mean studying or reading more. It is appreciating that prepping ourselves for it is just as important as the technique and effort. Shorter bursts of study, strategic naps for consolidation, sufficient sleep, and regular exercise are just as important for learning effectively as understanding, reading, writing what we learned, testing ourselves on it, and teaching others. Generally, for studying, the approach that is short, frequent, and reptitive tends to beat the one that is long, occasional, and novel.

Learning is generally a pleasant experience. But the tragedy of expecting abuse as a price for education can be avoided, as long as we stay mindful that learning does not have to be involve any such psychological mistreatment and that it can be done with anyone or no one, anytime and anywhere but is best done by ourselves, and it should be a subject to continual refinement. Seen in this light, there should be no need for scolding or shouting in order for learning to take place.

Now, having said all that, I feel we need to acknowledge that although abuse is not the optimal way to learn, there is a great deal we can learn from being in an incredibly challenging situation. Not all things, and certainly not *all* important things, can be learned from the comfort and security of a benign environment.

Just as there is no good without bad, no right without wrong, and no light without dark, being subject to a challenging environment is necessary to truly complete our education. It may sound harsh, but it was the experience of many of my predecessors and peers in our early years of legal practice in the late-90s and early-2000s.

Unlike the present generation, our seniors didn't concern themselves with our legal education development back then. They were also less mindful of the finer points of pleasantries when speaking to their subordinates.

As juniors then, we followed, observed, and learned what we could from being brought along by our seniors. Since they didn't explain the ordeal or tutor us, we merely had the opportunity and privilege to follow them closely in how they went about their work. Our education lay in those close observations and reflections. It was left to us to sift through the husk of emotions or events to get at the seed of learning and improve our abilities.

Those around and before my generation learned mostly by trial and error, as only a few books and fewer legal courses were accessible back then. The internet was still in its infancy, as far as its use in law and legal practice was concerned. Our errors were a painful but quick way to learn, because judges did not mince their words in those days. That privilege, instead, was only reserved for us.

But here's the thing: even though I did suffer a certain degree of 'abuse' in my practice, I did not regret that experience. Yes, it was tough; it was difficult. Sometimes, I even thought it was the end of my legal career. But, over time, through reflection, I have come to appreciate what those difficult moments did for me.

They shaped me.

Those difficult moments brought into sharp focus who I was, what my values were, and what I would do if I had the opportunity to impose my values and principles. It even clarified and solidified who I was and who I wanted to be.

That is why, even though it is not ideal, I feel there is some value to being in very demanding situations—we tend to find ourselves. I'm not saying we should actively seek out a needlessly 'abusive' situation or remain in one, but that being in one forces us to get clarity about the kind of lawyers we are, and what we seek from our legal practice. Such a situation forces us, inevitably, to build resilience, tenacity, and a thick hide—if we survive it, that is.

A part of me cannot help but feel that the present generation of lawyers loses out on valuable lessons because they tend to not go through the difficult experiences those of my generation, and the one before me, went through. I believe they lose out on the learnings and resilience that come from navigating a challenging, if not brutal, environment.

But, in fairness, their era is unlike mine. It is unreasonable to expect them to have the same experiences and come to possess the same values or principles. The litigation landscape now is much more benign and accommodating than it was back when I started practice.

Despite being through that difficult experience, I have never vetted it out on my colleagues. The experience I try to create for them—that is, benign, *sans* aggression or drama—is not what I was put through. I create for them the experience and environment I wish I had seen for myself when I was younger.

Yet, even though I do not encourage or inflict 'abuse', I respect those who come into the profession and are committed, despite their expectation of eventually having to put up with some of it without complaint, to thrive in our profession. They recognize that we cannot prepare a final draft without going through a few working ones first.

'Boss, How Come I Say the Same Thing, but You Get It and I Don't!'

My colleague said this to me the other day after we completed an online case management. In the recent sessions he had attended alone, he could not prevent applications that were filed after ours from being heard first, despite our application being filed earlier and dealing with a threshold issue of the case.

His exasperated remark was true. What I asked for was exactly what he had requested in an earlier session. We had discussed strategy and worked out tactics several times, our correspondence and recordings confirmed that. Yet, it boiled down to who had said it, rather than what was said. I empathized with him because I knew exactly how that felt.

His remark sent me down memory lane to my early years of practice, sometime in my first or second year. Back then, I went to court daily for matters, mostly mentions and simple hearings. There were occasions when my then-boss, Izzat, would come down to the Kuala Lumpur subordinate courts for the bigger, more complicated, or trickier matters.

I relished whenever that happened because it was an opportunity to watch, listen, and learn from him.

Whenever he came down, I would tell him about our problematic files, those stuck in court for weeks or months without progress. Back when I started, cases not being listed, cases listed but with missing files, or cases not updated with the latest filed documents, were regular occurrences that I had to contend with every time I went to court. When my efforts to remedy the situation, by way of letter or pleading with the counter clerks at the subordinate court's registry, failed (you thought lawyers only plead in courts, eh?), I had to bring in the boss.

There was one time he came with me to sort out some problematic files at the sessions court registry. It was located on the top floor of the Jalan Raja courthouse. Behind the Plexiglas counter, sat a lady clerk in a tudung and baju kurung, bearing an uninterested, indifferent look. I was familiar with her, as well as her look and facial configuration. Truthfully, whoever sat there did not matter because they all had the same look and attitude. She was consistently, patently dismissive and occasionally rude to me, in addition to being disinterested and slow.

Often, I waited hours for an unlisted file to be found and fixed again for mention the next day. Each time I asked for progress (with long intervals in between), she (and anyone who manned the counter) would rebuff me curtly by saying that I would be called if it was found. Oh, and if she did not call me, it meant it wasn't found. *Whowp-pish.*

Those were the growing pains in my early years of legal practice: being thoroughly disrespected and dismissed by the court counter clerks. Once the court computerization initiative was implemented, their immense blocking powers began to quickly fade before vanishing completely. This was good for efficiency and reduced opportunities for corruption. But I digress.

Izzat ambled up to the counter with a disarming smile, greeting her with a salam. She responded to him in a far different tone than I was accustomed to. During my many hours there, I often wondered whether she was capable of any tone other than disdain. Her attention was directed solely at my boss, completely ignoring me, even though I was next to him: literally, *right next to him*.

Now, the thing about Izzat was that he had first-class PR skills. He was the kind of person who could convince an Eskimo to buy a three-door freezer. A kampung boy from Kedah, who had come to the city and done well for himself, he had an uncanny natural ability to build rapport with people quickly and convincingly. It did not matter how high or low that person stood in society—he was good at reading people and figuring them out. It was Izzat who taught me that reading people is as important as reading the law because the law is ultimately about people.

Now, back to the grumpy lady.

After exchanging greetings, our conversation went more or less like this in Malay:

'How are you this morning, Cik?'

'Good. Healthy. Alhamdulillah. And just to correct you, I am a Puan, not Cik.'

'I am so sorry about that, Puan. I am Izzat. May I know your name?'

'Zaiton.'

'Thank you Puan Zaiton. Can I tell you something?'

'What is it?'

'You are looking good today. Your husband is a lucky man to have such a beautiful young wife like you.'

She was surprised and flattered.

'Eh, thank you, lah. But I am not so young anymore. I have two kids already, lah, Encik Izzat.'

'If you did not tell me, I would not have known. If you ask me, I would think you had gotten married recently; and if I didn't believe you, I would ask for proof!'

By then, the hint of a smile that crept up the sides of her mouth had seized control of her entire face, her cheeks turned a shade redder.

'Eh, no lah. But thank you. You are too kind. What can I do for you today?'

The conversation was cringy and corny, the kind I rolled my eyes at when I listened to it. I couldn't imagine having the temerity to say such things. But, bloody hell, it worked.

She lapped it up. And that was the first time Izzat had met her.

After he told her about our problematic cases, she asked him to sit and wait while she sorted them out. I saw her immediately leave her station, scurrying here and there. When it came to me, I never saw her move. In less than twenty minutes, she had located a few 'missing' files and relisted two matters for mention. This led me to realize that whenever I arrived, the counter folks couldn't give a damn about my requests. I stared at my boss with a mixture of disbelief and frustration.

To me, what he pulled off was magic: black, white, purple—I don't know—but it was magic. I saw the whole thing, and I still don't know what went down. He accomplished what had taken me weeks and months, not to mention writing letters and begging, in less than half an hour. This was an example of the 'junior experience' young lawyers faced during my time.

The next time I was there, Puan Zaiton was manning the counter again. I thought I would take the same approach, as I remembered the lines Izzat used.

'Assalamualaikum Puan Zaiton.'

'Salam.'

'How are you this morning?'

'Unh,' she grunted.

'You are looking good today.'

It came out half-hearted. I admit I lacked confidence—this was not my style. I was too scared to utter it, but nonetheless, gave it a shot. Instead of the warm reception I had hoped for, Puan Zaiton's eyes narrowed even more, and her mouth drew itself into a straight line.

'What is it?' she asked in her usual tone of disdain.

Whatever mound of courage I had built up to that point was smashed. I meekly gave her the list of unlisted and missing cases and quickly retreated to the safety of chairs across the counter. Like always, I waited for hours. Not a drop of the goodwill Izzat had fostered with her fell upon me. None. It was no different from any other time I was there.

When I got back to the office and met with him, I lamented. 'Uncle Izzat, how is it I say the same thing as you, but you get it and I don't?!'

He laughed. 'Those are things you cannot learn in the book of law, Fahri. You need experience for that.'

I have since understood that in law, as in life, who says it, how it is said, and when it is said are just as important, if not more, than what is said. This is not to say that words are not important. But, sometimes, they are not as crucial as we make them out to be. Also, we should best use our own words instead of others', because what worked for them may not work for us.

Hanging with the Seniors

I notice these days that pupils, interns, and fresh lawyers don't hang out with seniors, even when they have the opportunity to. If they do, they don't end up staying for long and politely excuse themselves on the account of work or something else.

I understand that ramblings of my peers can be dismissed as old uncle talk and, therefore, not worth sitting around for.

When I was a young lawyer, I relished the opportunity to sit with my seniors—the wrinklier, the better. I drew great pleasure from their tales of courtroom adventures, improbable close calls, against-all-odds cases, and magnificent should-have-won-'ems.

But only for the first time.

More importantly, I appreciated the treasures buried in their tales: their distillation of an area of law, exposition of a legal issue, unique approach to the law, and insights into legal practice reaped from battle-scarred legal experiences. There is much to be learned from our seniors' casual, seemingly meandering, circular conversations or discussions.

Of course, the volume of treasures contained varies from conversation to conversation, and much of it also depends on the people in the conversation. Expecting a motherlode each time is to harbour unreasonable expectations: It's closer to panning for gold. Even if the nuggets are small, they are still valuable.

Those buried treasures are there to be unearthed. We can only do so by keeping quiet and listening—really listening—and reflecting as we follow what they are talking about.

We can only listen. There will be no sign, cue, or mobile phone application to alert us when a valuable segment of the conversation is about to take place. They are not going to stop mid-conversation, seize your attention, and nudge you, 'Excuse me, you might want to pay attention to what we are about to discuss because it's going to be useful for you.'

It is entirely for us to discover.

Yes, we may ask them directly, but that is a treasure of a different nature. This, however, is of the teacher–student, senior–junior variety.

The treasure I am interested in comes from conversations between senior peers ranging a diversity of areas in which both are equally conversant and speaking their minds, unrestrained. What is dared to be said and thought in the igloo of privacy is exhilarating and far more insightful.

I call them treasures because it is knowledge that will never be captured between pages. They are also incapable of being compressed into a meme or a gif. We won't find them streamed or repeated on social media or media sites. Neither can they be recorded for later viewing.

These insights, wrought from deep experience and understanding, can only be passed on by engaging in conversation or witnessing its expression. We *have* to be there; we must be there to identify, unearth, and make sense of it. No one else can do it for us.

Yes, I concede some conversations are truly boring and of no value but that is the price we pay to sit through those worth our time.

Sometimes, and with some things, especially important, meaningful ones, there is no cheap, convenient, and efficient way to do it.

Not everything can nor should be reduced to those three commercial qualities.

Going Up Against a Senior

Going up against a senior lawyer is often a daunting and stressful experience, especially so when we are fresh. The anxiety remains despite the seniority. It lies in the apparent gulf of experience, reputation, and learning between the senior and ourselves. It has a touch of David and Goliath to it.

Even for someone with my seniority, that is, twenty years and up at the Bar, which I think of as middling seniority, there are occasions when I experience a spot of anxiety while going up against a more senior lawyer. The difference between then and now is merely the management of anxiety, which is far better today.

Some may be of the opinion that more than twenty years at the Bar is a long time. In that case, why do I consider myself of middling seniority?

This is how I see it: Say we start our career as advocates and solicitors at twenty-five years of age. A Malaysian person's average life expectancy, presently, is seventy-six years old. Assuming we live and practice law that long, I'd peg a full career at the Bar to be at fifty years, more or less.

So, over twenty years is about halfway to the finish line.

We must be careful about using duration at the Bar as a proxy indicator of a lawyer's competency, credibility, and courage—because it is not. Your time at the Bar simply indicates the number of years you have existed as a licensed lawyer in

Malaysia. While it may imply that you have actively been in practice, accumulated the necessary and relevant experience, continually improved your ability, and are competent at what you do, but years at the Bar are not guaranteed indicators of any of that.

Years at the Bar don't matter if you haven't accomplished anything meaningful with them; what we do with those numbers is what counts. Never be fooled by raw numbers, for some lawyers have been at the Bar longer than me, but their practice still reeks of rawness. These are who we call the 'senior freshies'.

Not all senior lawyers achieve the level of ability, experience, knowledge, courage, and competency expected of them, given their respective seniority. There is a spectrum of quality to senior lawyers, ranging from appallingly bad to magnificently good. Their rarity mirrors their ability: the bad ones are common, the great less so. There will always be this quality spectrum any time we categorize lawyers according to any criteria.

When I say going up against a senior lawyer, I mean those on the latter end of the scale. When I say senior lawyer, I mean the heavies, the big kahunas, the goombas with the heavy rep sheet. Those with the litany of groundbreaking cases, the ear of the bench, the brilliant arguments, the deft strategies, and the command of authority. The ones who were cutting their teeth while we were still soiling and wetting our diapers. Those who make us tremble and soil or wet our robes from their gravitas.

They are much like the ultimate bad boss in a video game, the ones you have to play and lose several times to, before figuring out the strategy to beat them, which, even when you do, would be barely managed. These senior lawyers have an eloquent and elegant response to everything—they know all our law-fu moves and their counters. They pull checkmates out of their arse.

These are the kind of people I imply, when I say 'going up against a senior'.

On the other hand, there is no glory or pleasure in going up against a senior freshie. They are often an embarrassment to our profession: much like the illegitimate child everyone knows about but are embarrassed to acknowledge. Senior freshies elicit more pity than argument, and their performances are commonly a masterclass of what not to do.

We may watch them for either education or amusement—preferably, both. Savour how they spin an argument out of their ignorance of both facts and law. Regale in how quickly they resort to ad hominem[26] attacks. Marvel at the madness of their arguments. Be awed by their appalling, spoiled-brat behaviour, which the court countenances, if not encourages, solely because of their years at the Bar. Some of them even think being angry is an argument.

I once defended a hospital against a medical negligence claim. We acted for the hospital, which had been sued vicariously for an allegedly negligent diagnosis by its doctor. In most cases, the claimant has to bring some expert evidence to prove a negligent misdiagnosis: You need a doctor to explain to the court why the doctor got it wrong. You cannot simply bring medical results and ask the court to infer the negligence. However, that's what precisely happened.

On the day of trial, before the hearing ensued, the claimant's very senior lawyer boasted to me he would prove the negligence without any expert evidence. 'This case is very clear,' he said. I thought he was foolhardy, if not ignorant.

[26] Personal attacks against the lawyer

But it was neither my case, nor my problem. 'I look forward to that, Dato,' I replied.

He lost badly. The court ruled that his client has been unable to prove a case in court.

In the first year of my practice, I was introduced by a lawyer friend to a senior. It was in the old Jalan Raja Criminal Magistrates' Court, where the lawyer himself had formerly been a Magistrates' Court prosecuting officer for donkey years. He was a short, dark, curly-haired man with more showmanship than substance. I remember what he boasted about to me because I was obsessed with books.

'I am the type of lawyer that doesn't read books. Who needs them? You waste time reading books,' he had claimed. 'Everything I learn is from observation. A real lawyer is one that uses his mouth. You *kena pandai cakap*[27]! Ha! The judge listens to those that pandai cakap.'

I am pretty sure I looked at him askance. I never sought him out for anything. Both these instances are my parables about critically considering what senior lawyers (actually, anyone) tell us about our profession, especially when we don't know any better. If it doesn't square with our first principles (for example, mine being that reading is good, and *not reading* is *not good*), we must treat it with great caution; if not, we must outright reject it.

I remember how anxious, nervous, and stressed out I was, when pitted against a senior lawyer in the early years of my practice. It would drive me to intensify my preparations.

If I were going up against my peer, I would read an authority once or twice. But if it were a senior lawyer, I would read it at least three or four times. I would be mentally sweating and

[27] *Pandai cakap* is Malay slang for 'speaking intelligently or cleverly'.

physically fidgeting a bit more on the hearing day. I remember my hands or legs trembling when I was on my feet. The worst part was the sense of dread that used to fill me.

This dread and its intensification are distractions from getting our work done. But they can be managed.

The first is to focus on your case, points, and arguments.

Remember, you are there to make your point and, then, sit down. As long as you have made your point to the judge, your job as a lawyer is done. A trial or hearing is not pageantry for lawyers personally, but their arguments for their clients. The court decides who has the better argument, not who the better lawyer is. The judge is interested in the soundness of your argument and the quality of your evidence, not your personal qualities.

If and when you feel dread, a lack of confidence, or cluelessness about managing your emotions, return to familiarizing yourself with your arguments or rehearsing them.

Focusing on your case reduces the time you spend thinking about who you are going up against. Filling our heads and attention with our arguments helps reduce anxiety about our situation. The senior lawyer is not cavorting with and dominating your thoughts, which leaves less room for the darkness of our minds to whittle away at our confidence with negative thoughts.

Next, avoid paying attention to how you think you look, when you do what you do.

Much of our anxiety and dread stems from our negative self-perception when going up against a senior lawyer. We tend to think we will perform poorly and embarrass ourselves, fearing the senior lawyer will slay our case with their ability and argument. There is apprehension that judges will dub us as shysters for raising poor arguments, and the list goes on and on. Our mind often continually generates many ways in which we will lose and embarrass ourselves.

We must train ourselves to avoid these thoughts or to distract ourselves from them, as they do nothing but subtract from our performance.

Not everything we think is good for us; this is one of those times. A helpful way to do that is to return to the first instruction.

These two actions have helped me deal with the dread and intensification of effort when going up against a senior lawyer. You may find them of use.

Taking Chances

A second-year law student once asked me in an email interview, 'If you did not want to hire me, what could I do to change your mind?'

That question ended up being interesting to answer.

I immediately replied, 'I don't know, but it would have to be very persuasive.'

I was about to leave it at that when, suddenly, the answer dawned upon me. My lawyer, Ameerul Aizat, had answered this question a few years ago. Him ending up as a lawyer in my firm is an interesting story I enjoy recounting, particularly when citing an example of passion and sacrifice for learning and experience.

The backdrop to our first encounter occurred in 2015, when I was cynical about relying solely on the resume and interview process to select candidates—be it for hiring associates, pupils, or interns. Given this doubt, I resorted to the crude method of choosing candidates for whimsical reasons.

So, when Aizat sent his application to the firm, I immediately took him on, solely because of his name. I did not even read his resume and cover letter—that happened only after I accepted his offer. My logic for taking him on was the firm's name: Azzat & Izzat. His name, Aizat, includes the first two letters of the partner's names and shares the same last three letters. Thus, it seemed fitting for him to join us as a pupil. While some may view this as whimsical, I think of it as creating conditions for serendipity.

He wrote back to ask if there was an interview, to which I replied in the negative. He was instructed to report for work on a specified date, because there were already two pupils working under me at the time.

When he began, he had my father, Azzat, as his master. I found that arrangement as amusing as it was fitting. Aizat later followed me as a pupil in 2016, when I left my father's firm to set up my own. He was the first ever pupil of mine to have both my father and me as his master.

Initially, when he joined me, I confessed to him, and this other pupil of mine, Mohd Fitri, that I would not be retaining them, owing to case and budget constraints. While the firm already had three lawyers, there was neither enough paid work nor clients. I definitely had no room at all for a fourth and fifth lawyer. In this nascent environment, Aizat completed his pupillage with me sometime by the end of April 2016, four months after I set up my firm.

In his last week, Aizat asked me out for a *teh tarik* at Restoran Al-Madina, our nearby mamak, for a chat and to hear my thoughts about some of the options he had been considering after his call to the Bar. A few sips of tea later, Aizat launched into his options. He began by telling me that he was considering a Master's degree because his then-fiancée now-wife was moving overseas for the same, and he was not averse to doing one to accompany her.

I agreed. 'It makes sense if you have the money for it,' I replied.

However, he did not intend to spend any more money on education just yet and wanted to start earning. He told me he might join the Attorney General's Chambers, as he had some friends there.

I remember saying it was a good option, as the experience there would be different from the private sector. He would learn the government side of things and eventually translate that into private practice after he left. Moreover, having friends there would make acclimatizing easier and quicker.

But there was another catch: He did not want to be posted anywhere else, something that was beyond his control. Plus, he felt he wasn't ready for a large organization, never mind the government. The plan to begin private practice and applying to a small legal firm was another consideration.

I responded in the positive for that idea too, for I have always felt private practice gives one plenty of room to try out other things besides legal practice. That is, if done properly and productively, of course.

However, he wanted to be assured of the flexibility of practising criminal law and the opportunities to do so in a diversity of legal areas.

At last, he finally arrived at the point I had sensed he was leading up to: He wanted me to consider taking him on as a legal assistant, offering to agree to a minimum wage, which would be paid as per my affordability. In case the firm landed in a tough spot, he would voluntarily leave. Then, I could repay as and when I had sufficient funds.

It was an incredibly generous offer. But there was more.

'How long is this deal supposed to be?' I asked.

'A year,' he said. Though I thought it was risky, he assured me that his parents had agreed to support him during that time. Even though I felt a year was too long a time and unfair to him, I agreed to try it for six months and gauge where we got.

Finally, we agreed to pay him a fraction of his six-month wage and that if I could pay him the unpaid portion after the same time period, we would continue working together.

What came through loud and clear from his incredibly generous offer was his firm belief that my foetal firm was a fertile field for him to grow his talents. He seemed convinced about learning something worthwhile with me. Above all, he was willing to 'go hungry' for that experience—an attitude I have a lot of respect for because it mirrors my own. Moreover, by that time, I had a favourable opinion of his abilities and was convinced of his potential. Lastly, the boldness and thoughtful nature of his offer assured me that he not only thought differently but also was someone worth taking a risk on and investing in.

We shook hands on it and proceeded. Many of my acquaintances have told me that it was unreasonable to have that many lawyers, given how nascent my firm and how meagre my clientele was.

One time, a senior lawyer subtly told me that he never had more than two lawyers under him at any given point, hearing which, I grew less confident about my decision. I reassured myself that if I was going to make mistakes, it was best to make as many of them as early as possible.

Towards the end of Aizat's first month, I realized how vastly different I would end up paying him, compared to others. I felt awful about it: if at all he were lazy and recalcitrant, this wouldn't be the case because an excuse would be handy. But he was diligent, thoughtful and, as I said, 'hungry'. This was one of those acute moments where I felt I was faced with the choice of following what I *felt*—paying him fully, despite our agreement—as opposed to what I *thought*, being prudent with the finances, and paying him as per our agreement.

After much hand-wringing, I broke our pact and paid him his full wages. Prudence be damned! We will all have to work harder to see where we get! After the move, I was pleased with myself, even though faint sense of 'what the hell am I doing?' lingered.

After receiving his pay, Aizat sought to speak with me.

'I think there is a mistake,' he said. 'You overpaid me.'

'No. I didn't,' I replied. 'I am paying you what I should be paying you.'

'But can you manage?'

'We will,' I said, more out of hope than conviction.

We continued to work together until Aizat's seventh year of practice, when he departed to open up his own firm. During that time, Aizat and I were called together on the same day as Syarie Counsels for Wilayah Persekutuan in June 2018 and moved by our then-colleague, Farhan Haziq.

Our years together were a privilege and a pleasure. I enjoyed watching him grow from strength to strength in a diversity of areas. He is a diligent, versatile, organized, intelligent, and efficient lawyer who is relentlessly gaining competency in areas of law that interest him.

Even today, we have a lot of fun discussing legal issues, working on cases and testing out arguments. The only difference now is that we do so from our own respective firms. I am pleased and grateful we both took a chance on each other and gained mutually from it. Aizat was a happy occasion of taking a chance on someone.

To me, this is what practice should be all about—practising the law, working on cases as best we can, and enjoying it with people who want to work the same way. This naturally leads to better quality work, something that contented lawyers produce. Although, to reach there, we have to take risks, even if they cannot be justified for at that time, because the foundations of our decisions are mostly just a hunch and wee bit of hope.

So, now, here is my answer:

Question: If you did not want to hire me, what could I do to change your mind?

I respond to this with another question: What would you be willing to give up for an opportunity to change my mind?

A Burst of Laughter in the Office

I was in the second year of running my firm on my own. It was a weekday afternoon: maybe around three, I don't remember the day. There was a stillness in the air.

I was standing at my desk, typing away intently, when I heard a burst of collective riotous laughter rip through the quiet. It came from the room next door, where four of my lawyers sat in their respective cubicles in what was then our office area.

It was not unusual to occasionally hear laughter from the office area waft into my room. But that day, it was particularly loud and went on for a bit. From timbre and texture of the sound, I figured it must have been something really funny.

Even though the laughter ebbed, it grated me as I worked. The more I thought about it, the greater the grating grew.

Here I am, working, while my lawyers are laughing in the room next door. Hell, I don't even get to hear the damn joke. This is completely out of line. There should be no more laughing during office hours! Lawyers should only work—and because our work is serious, the environment should be too. They are not here for fun and games. I am not paying them to come to the office to have a good time.

By the time I finished my thought, I was thoroughly annoyed. I was going to go over and give them a piece of my mind.

I moved from my table, took a deep breath, and blew air out of my nose to brace myself for the encounter. Then, I took another, followed by two more. Instead of being energized to go over, a different thought swam to me.

What's wrong with a bout of laughter between colleagues? Isn't that a good thing, an indicator that they get along? It suggests things are well between them, as those who laugh together enjoy each other's company. And doesn't the sound of laughter cast a warm glow over the office environment? Doesn't it leave everyone with a fuzzy, feel-good feeling? That's what I want, right? A warm, cozy, feel-good environment? Laughter is a good thing. Don't go over there and poach a good thing. Why do you want to do a stupid thing like that?

That stopped me in my tracks. I felt the annoyance and anger dissipate.

I walked back to my desk and continued my work.

I often reflected on that moment of restraint afterwards. Looking back, I recognized it as one of those tiny, pivotal moments of my life that have significantly impacted my approach to the environment I wanted to create in the office. I also figured out what those two feelings and voices represented for me.

The first feeling was that of the old-school, senior lawyer attitude I was not unfamiliar with. Such bosses generally expected lawyers to be at their beck and call, and could not help but infer that we were playing truant whenever we were not in the office. It was understood that we were at work not to have fun, but to keep quiet and do our work efficiently. Stay late, if need be, but still arrive on time in the morning. Our opinions should be oriented towards confirming their views instead of advancing our own.

As the same senior boss's son, I received it to a much lesser degree, of course, but I was nonetheless sensitive to it. I saw and heard, over the years, how it was for others.

The second voice, even though, had a counterintuitive feel to it, but the more I thought about it, the more attuned it was to my outlook of how things should be. These moments of shared pleasure between colleagues are important building blocks to a warm and efficient work relationship. They complement and ornament conversations between colleagues, often being the drops of glue that better bond relationships.

The greater the frequency, quality, and openness of communication between us, the better the quality of our relationships. Quality relationships are the foundation on which trust is built. It is from such webs of trusted relationships that we achieve real efficiency.

When we trust each other, things move quickly. There are fewer barriers to communication. We deal with each other plainly, instead of strategically, and anticipate instead of suspect each other. Trust creates room and space to confess to each other our errors and failures, instead of hiding them. It also builds the foundation for a full and frank discussion, making it is easier to encourage spontaneous order and effective efficiency with trust.

Since then, I let the days go by as they should. I have learned to appreciate the sound of laughter in the office. Whether it is between colleagues or with a client, it doesn't matter. I welcome and encourage it, for I love having a laugh every day—several, if possible. And I'm talking about those laugh-out-loud, quiet-busting, thigh-slapping, belly-trembling kinds of laughs—you know, the big ones. It does not matter whether I am the cause or consequence of it.

It is very important that we all have a good laugh together to create a welcoming, warm, and efficient office environment. Hell, it just makes the day more fun. A day punctuated with laughter feels like a day out with friends, making the workplace feel much less like an office and more like a den for friends.

Dressing for Work

At the firm atelier, the lawyers have a dynamic but relaxed dress code. What we must wear depends on what we have scheduled for the day.

If we have no court attendance or client meetings that day, we come in casuals. Slacks, jeans, shirts, T-shirts , collared, with or without a shirt, dresses, baju kurung, whatever—it's fine. However, only shorts and risqué wear require prior approval.

We allow it because I like dressing casually for days in the office when I don't have to see anyone formally, that is, no meetings with clients, no appointments, hearings or trials in court. It's for those days when we are focused on the backroom work like drafting, crafting, thinking, strategizing, or responding to emails.

Although we dress up for show, we dress down for flow.

The principle for casual dressing is that no matter how casual, it should be informed by a sense of decorum, appropriateness and a semblance of style. Casual does not mean sloppy, but comfortable and with character. Stylish is encouraged and appreciated, provided it is not flashy or loud.

If we have a meeting with clients at the office, smart casual is the minimum. If we have a meeting at a corporate client's office, or at government department, we get the armour of a black three-piece suit, white shirt, dark tie, and black leather shoes for gents; and a fitting, well-cut black jacket, white shirt, black skirt/pants and shoes for the ladies.

I eschew a jacket at times. Despite its absence, I like to think the presence of a tie and vest allows me to meet the lowest acceptable threshold of formality.

If we have a hearing or trial, naturally, we are attired appropriately.

For open court, a collar, bands, a white shirt, a black short jacket, black-grey striped pants, and a black linen robe are appropriate. For High Court chamber hearings and subordinate court matters, a black suit, a white shirt, and a quiet tie is what I stick to. We cannot, and should not, be flashy or showy with our court dress nor are we meant to be. Our sombre uniformity of dress is supposed to symbolize how we, as advocates, differ little from each other, with distinctions only existing in the quality of arguments we advance.

What I said about the court earlier, applies only if we're going for a 'physical hearing' or 'physical trial'—going to court is referred to as such these days. For someone practising as long as I have been (circa 1999), I find those phrases disconcerting and ominous . If we are in an online hearing, not all I mentioned applies because dressing waist up is all that is required. We may lose the shoes and pants if we feel like, but it should go no further than that.

The reason we have such a dress code is because I personally like having such flexibility, including the comfort and pleasure derived from it. I don't see why such a code cannot extend to my colleagues, so long as they are sensible and responsible about it, which I know them to be.

A flexible dress code gives me the opportunity to wear my other clothes. I remember, back in the day, when I wore black and white every day. I had to attend court most days of the week. Even when I didn't, I wore it just in case I had to visit. Many of my clothes and other coloured suits hanging in the cupboard were neglected. When I finally got around to wearing them, they didn't fit well anymore.

What's more, I get to choose what I want to wear and dress comfortably. My eccentricity has another safe outlet to express itself.

There are days when I don't see anyone but dress up anyway. Days when I turn up in what my colleagues call my guru outfit: opaque loose-fitting white linen pants and shirt with either a white or black sleeveless singlet. There are the occasional black T-shirt and jeans days too. It is nice to be able to wear the more eccentric stuff to work. It's also interesting to see what others at the firm choose to wear on days they don't have to dress formally.

Interestingly, because of the freedom to dress as I please, I have a stronger sense of occasion when dressing up for my open court hearing or trial, whatever the court hierarchy level may be. To me, our formal attire serves as an ever-present reminder to be professional in court and to abide by our professional ethical code.

Just because we have to work doesn't mean we have to always look like it. Whenever the occasion calls for formality, of course, we should rise to meet it, for we cannot have it our way all the time. But when no such compulsions outweigh us, and when we are with our colleagues working closely together, there should be fewer formal encumbrances.

GROWING UP AND ABOUT LEGALLY

'Sit Near the Staff'

My mother insisted on this before I began my pupillage at my father's firm in 1998.

She did not approve of the firm's arrangement, where the bosses, lawyers, and pupils sat upstairs near the library, but the other staff—comprised of the receptionist, clerks, and dispatch—sat downstairs.

'Sit near the staff. There is no one supervising them downstairs, because of which they do as they please,' she had told me. 'Whenever I call the office, either no one picks up or they take forever. On the few occasions I go there, I find them chatting and not doing their work. Hopefully, they will be more diligent when the boss's son sits downstairs. So, sit near the staff. And don't tell Dad I asked you to sit downstairs!'

'Of course, Mom,' I assured her.

Let me give you the backdrop to this. As the boss' son, everyone at the firm knew where I was supposed to sit, even before I had arrived. There were five rooms on the first floor: the two closest to the office frontage were taken by the bosses, my father and Izzat; the one beside my father's room was taken by a lawyer named Rose. The room beside Izzat's was reserved for me. The last and biggest room on the first floor served as the library.

Even though my room had a table, chair, a phone line, and shelves, it had been empty for years, as no one was allowed to occupy the room. It was reserved solely for me. I had the privilege of occupying it during my pupillage—something my peers could not get because the rooms are meant only for lawyers.

I told my father I wanted the empty cubicle downstairs, which lay at the back of the office. At the time, it was used as storage space because it had been unoccupied. He found this request strange but indulged me.

However, for me, it was a strategic choice. There were three main areas downstairs: the reception, the office area, and the storage area. The ratio of each of the respective areas was 1:5, 3:5, and 1:5. I had a view of the office and the storage area but not the reception, which was enough because all the staff were stationed there, save for the receptionist.

Once I sat in that cubicle, the party was over for them. During my first month there, I recalled the first four lines of the first stanza of Yeats' 'The Second Coming':

> Turning and turning in the widening gyre
> The falcon cannot hear the falconer;
> Things fall apart; the centre cannot hold;
> Mere anarchy is loosed upon the world . . .[28]

The staff were well-behaved for the first week or so but fell apart after, lapsing to their old ways. I saw how late the dispatch boys came to the office, heard the accounts clerk's constant chatter while seated at her desk with the other clerk across the room, saw the litigation clerks call up their children

---

[28] Yeats, W.B. (1989) The Second Coming, Poetry Foundation. Available at: https://www.poetryfoundation.org/poems/43290/the-second-coming (Accessed: 16 December 2024).

and spouses, witnessed the conveyancing clerks leave the office as they pleased, and a whole lot more. I was appalled at how outrageous the situation was. It is not easy to keep up a daily pretence of work without the vice of habit.

Watching them work *was* work. With the 'office machinery' now laid bare to me, I could see the gears were faulty, rusty, and in dire need of an overhaul. Just to give a sense of the timelines they worked with: A senior litigation clerk took a week to draw up a substituted service application. This was a simple document to serve court papers by advertisement in the newspapers. I could do it in fifteen minutes! Needless to say, almost all of the staff disliked me and thought I was a pain in the ass.

After I completed my pupillage, I requested for my cubicle area to be converted into a partitioned room, so I could maintain vigilance over the staff whilst shoring up some privacy for myself. I eventually got rid of all but two of the employees, and hired new ones to fill the vacancies. I also gave up the room reserved for me.

Since then, it has been is a habit of mine to choose a room next to the staff area. Experience helps me appreciate the wisdom of my mother's advice and the benefits that flow from it. Aside from better supervision, sitting close to the staff gives me more opportunities to interact with them, making for closer and more meaningful relationships.

But if I were to choose where to sit, I would prefer it to be just how it had been back when I first set up my firm in 2016: a few tables and abandoned chairs left by the previous tenant arranged to form a square in a room in which I sat around with my lawyers and pupils. We had no staff then—we all took turns as staff—it was not comfortable or luxurious, and the furniture was crap. But what I liked the best about that arrangement was our working hours would inevitably be punctuated with impromptu conversations, discussions, and laughter throughout the day. In the evening, when I left the office, there a sense of having spent the day with friends.

It is not the seat that matters, but who we choose to sit with.

'Forget About Client's Money'

This was my father's advice for me after I started my legal career. He gave it to every pupil that went through his firm. I don't know whether he still does it anymore, but I have carried on that tradition.

'Bank it [the client's money] in, note when to pay it out, then forget about it,' he had said. 'Those that keep looking at it, or thinking about it, get into trouble. Even if you go bankrupt or your family is starving, you cannot touch that money.'

For a long time, I understood his advice—though only in theory. I say, in theory because, for a long time, I was a mere legal assistant at my father's firm. I never made partner, never had to manage the client's account, never had to entertain clients, and never felt the weight of aggregated client monies in an account with my name on it.

'Clients' money' was but a theoretical construct. But I understood money, and what it did to people. Money warps people's perceptions, arouses greed, tempts, seduces—especially when it's other people's money.

'Some of these lawyers think they can use the clients' money quickly and then have it back before they have to pay it out. It's a gamble. Not a gamble you want to take. You want to gamble, you go to the casino,' my father explained. 'Why do you think banks don't often want to take on a sole proprietorship? They are scared some of these fly-by-night fellas get on their panel, get a big loan, pack up, and *cabut*[29] with the money.'

Here are two examples. In 2014, Herlina Khamisiah Sauli pleaded guilty to misusing RM 418,500 of her client's money that was supposed to be proceeds from the sale of a house and for misusing a further RM 261,000 clients' money.[30] In Singapore, 'veteran lawyer' Ooi Oon Tat was suspended in 2019 for a year for banking in Singapore $138,148 into his office account instead of his client's.[31]

There are many, many more.

Now that I run my own firm, I understand his advice through experience. I now hold funds for others, either while awaiting the completion of a property sale or pending a judgment sum during an appeal. And, oh boy, there is a lot of money. Thankfully, I do not have to hold those monies for long. My policy is to pay out the moment the triggering event happens. Why should I hold someone else's money a moment longer than I needs to?

The client is fully aware of the timeline for receiving their money. When they don't get it as per schedule, they get anxious, nervous, and suspicious. Latent or freshly minted suspicions about the trustworthiness of their lawyer materialize like a hidden ghost that reveals itself all of a sudden. The client's

---

[29] To pull or run away.

[30] Reduan, H. (2014) Real Estate Lawyer jailed: New Straits Times, NST Online. Available at: https://www.nst.com.my/news/2015/09/real-estate-lawyer-jailed (Accessed: 16 December 2024).

[31] Lum, S. (2022) Lawyer suspended 5 years for 'lackadaisical' conduct that caused client to lose case, The Straits Times. Available at: https://www.straitstimes.com/singapore/courts-crime/lawyer-suspended-5-years-for-lackadaisical-conduct-that-caused-client-to-lose-case (Accessed: 16 December 2024).

fevered fearful fits project fanciful fraudulent intentions on you, where none exist.

The best way to assure a client is to pay them when you are supposed to. Not before, because you may be liable for breaching an undertaking; but not a day after either, for that will make the client anxious and suspicious. If you sense a delay, inform your client that very moment and assure them of your fixing measures and the expected time window to receive the money.

Ever since setting up on my own firm, I have been implementing my father's advice scrupulously. Using the client's money is not the type of temptation you get rid of in the Wildean manner by yielding to it. This is the kind one resists by forgetting about it until the time arrives to relieve oneself of that responsibility.

In a world where we are constantly told that personal contentment is found by acquisition and accumulation, there is a subtle pleasure and relief in being able to deliberately forget some things, even if it is for only a little while.

Will I Ever Argue a Case of Some Importance?

In the first few years of practice, I found myself asking this question from time to time, when I ran the gamut of debt and traffic claims, and defences in the lower courts for the firm.

This question would come to me during those long, dull, and lonely waits. If not in the subordinate court registry, I'd be waiting in court, waiting for my case to be called up.

In the good old days, whatever we filed in the court registry, took ages to be sealed or find its way into the court file, if at all it did. If you filed something the day before the court date, forget about it being in the court file the next day. Either the application or affidavit would be missing or the court file altogether. The norm was to file them at least a week before the court date. But even then, there was no guarantee that it would be in the court file whenever the case was called up.

Since the digitalization of the courts, missing applications, affidavits, and files are a thing of the past. But back in the day, it was a regular and common occurrence, which explained why I was a regular and common visitor to the subordinate court registry.

In the days of yore, the subordinate court registry at the Jalan Raja courts was split into two. The first, Magistrates' Court registry, was located just inside the official entrance of the Jalan Raja courthouse buildings. The second half, Sessions Court registry, was on the third floor, if I am not mistaken. It was a long walk up.

I spent many hours of the morning (and sometimes the afternoon) under semi-bright fluorescent lights that casted their cold, indifferent light over the cheap-looking wooden partitions and transparent acrylic counter divider, waiting for lost applications and missing court files to be found. Sometimes, I waited for hours only to be told, '*Fail/permohonan tak jumpa. Tulis surat.*'[32] I often went back disgusted at having wasted a whole morning sitting around unproductively.

The work at the office did not get done while I waited in court.

This was a time before the ubiquity of mobile phones and laptops. If you didn't bring any entertainment to the courts, good luck passing the time if your friends weren't around. I was always prepared for the waiting part: I had my book, newspaper, notepad, pen, and files. Even though my entertainment tools were always close at hand, they sometimes failed to stem the relentless waves of boredom.

Back then, I waited so much in court, I began to joke that I wasn't a lawyer but a waiter. I waited for a mention date, a file to be located, an application to be called up, and to see court clerks and officers. There was always something to wait for.

In those lonely, futile moments, I wondered whether I would ever have the opportunity to argue a Federal Court or a Court of Appeal case, that is, a case in the superior courts. Never mind if it was insignificant, though any appellate court decision is not. Never mind the area of law. It didn't matter if I won or lost, I would just be happy to argue any case at that level.

---

[32] 'The file/application cannot be found. Write a letter.'

There were occasions when the anxiety of never having an opportunity gripped me. It seemed so far away from my daily work. I handled traffic accidents, debt claims, and defences, execution proceedings, petty crime, and routine, low-level litigation. I didn't see how kicking tenants out, auctioning off goods and suing debtors for their dues, never mind spending half my life at the court registries, would elevate me to the exalted heights of arguing fine ethereal points of law in the appellate courts.

I'd like to think I have come a long way from my early days, with more than twenty years' worth of practice.

These days, unlike my initial years, I don't take up routine legal work. I feel privileged and pleased to be called upon to be involved in interesting litigation and cases. There is hardly ever a dull moment or case. I am privileged to argue matters in the superior courts, not infrequently.

I don't know whether any decisions I was involved in were significant or influential—that doesn't matter so much to me these days. Anyway, those matters are not mine to declaim; they are for others and legal history to consider. I am simply there to argue the case as ably as I can, within my professional ethics, tradition, and abilities, and to savour the experience along the way in the company of my colleagues.

I want to share a few observations about my transition from legal grunt work in my early practice to conducting cases at the appellate level.

Firstly, it is not about how you start, but where you end. We all begin somewhere, and in a long-established profession with deep traditions like ours, it is inevitably at the bottom of the food chain. There is no shame in kicking things off from there, because it is the natural starting point—we don't have any experience nor do we know enough laws and people.

The shame, however, lies in never leaving the bottom.

I learned a lot there. Even though it quickly became drudgery because routine work tends to bore me, those years were important. I learned how to carry out service of documents, entering default judgments and setting them aside, and all kinds of applications. I learned the nitty gritty and the granules in between as well as a lot of useless stuff.

I learned the various ways to enforce judgments: how to bankrupt someone, wind up a company, sell their belongings or property, and evict tenants. It is just as important to know how to enforce a judgment as it is to obtain one. Although they are no longer at my fingertips, I can still feel them around my elbows.

All these basic, low-level, routine tasks later served me well throughout my career in practice and helped lay the foundation for my legal practice.

Second, develop your legal skill set and interest in the law.

Keep your head down and eyes open for the first five to seven years of legal practice. Focus like a spotlight on your work. Develop your legal skillset and practice relentlessly. Do the drafting, deal with clients, complete as many cases or transactions as you can on your own. Look for opportunities to learn from others. Experiment. Try stuff out.

Concern yourself simply with doing whatever you are given to the best of your abilities. Keep that intensity through your work. Make it an ethic.

Don't concern yourself with curating your work or work life on social media. Don't waste time trying to market or preen yourself for public consumption, unless you want to attract the kind of crowd that lives on social media. Don't compare yourself to others. We are all on unique, different trajectories in our lives.

Find or set up a firm to settle in with good work and get down to doing the work. Seize every piece of work like it was the only file you had. Believe that if you mess it up, you won't get any more work. When friends or colleagues call for help, oblige.

Find out as much as possible about whatever provision you are invoking and what procedure you need to use. Read the actual statutory or enactment provisions. Read the case law about it. Read around the subject. Go for courses. Ask your friend for guidance, but weight their answer.

Let your walk do the talk for you. Make others know that you are a sound and formidable lawyer through your work and conduct, not your own words. If at all words have to be there, let them be the words of others.

Quality always finds its way to the top, or close to it, because it is always appreciated. It is also scarce, and hence, stands out—especially next to mediocrity. Quality is irrepressible, and if you have cultivated it, don't worry. It is simply a matter of time.

Don't watch the time. Watch what you are doing and give it your best.

Third, patience.

A legal career is a long one. By my finger-in-the-wind estimation, we generally enter legal practice between the ages of twenty-three and twenty-six. If we take a full legal career to be fifty years long, that would take us to the ages between seventy-three and seventy-six. I am nearly halfway there, as I hit twenty-five years of legal practice next year.

On one hand, I can't believe it's been that long. On the other, I am in disbelief that there's still half a career in legal practice left, if I live that long. It feels like I have lived through at least two or three legal practice lifetimes since I began.

If you are in the legal profession for the long haul, work towards the long-term. Try more areas of law or deepen your interest in one. Refining your legal skillset takes practice, effort, and time. Lots of time. So, take time. Don't rush it. Having a mentor enriches and accelerates learning and provides opportunities.

All those things add up to your experience. Building a legal career based on a solid legal skillset sets us up for a long time in practice.

Don't worry if nobody knows you early on in your practice, for we all start that way. If you work smart and hard, and your work starts to speak for itself, others will notice and talk about it. Opportunities will appear. At the same time, find opportunities to do the kind of cases you are interested in. Or, at the least, imagine each case as the one you wanted to do.

Don't worry about taking your time.

Fourth, friends and comrades-in-cause.

Both are important for our mental, psychological, and legal well-being. They are there to console, inspire, support, and help us. They pick us up when we are down and raise us higher when we are up. We must extend the same grace to them.

A comrade-in-cause is someone in the trenches, struggling for the same cause as us. The comrades-in-cause comprehend, if not share, our disappointments and frustrations, including the legal arguments that go with them.

I would have left legal practice long ago, if I didn't have friends and comrades-in-cause. As much as I love and enjoy legal practice, I know that much of it is disappointing, enervating, disgusting, and hypocritical. Friends and comrades-in-cause are the balm to my encounters with those situations and people. They restore my faith in people and the law, reminding me that amid all the bad, there is still good, and we should strive for better.

Fifth, think organic.

I am not talking about the produce. I have in mind the nature of growth we should have about ourselves and the things around us.

Organic means 'developing in the manner of a living plant or animal'—that is, growing and developing naturally. Growth is not hurried, it is not forced, and its rate is incremental and modest. It is neither exponential nor artificial.

Whether personal or firm-wide, organic growth is sustainable over the long-term; it is slow but steady. It is much like taking a walk. Exponential growth looks exciting over the short-term, but rarely can we sustain it for long. Exponential growth runs very fast, before you even warm up. The inevitable hurt comes through later, when it fails in the long run because of its unnatural and, inevitably, dehumanizing nature.

Since a legal career is long, go organic. Take your time, as there is no hurry. Read things carefully, and, importantly, think things through. Explore what you don't know. Do not violate your integrity and that of others to get things done faster. You end up hurting only yourself in the end.

Those who seek rapid growth remind me of the drivers on the roads who try to overtake everybody. For all their overtaking, zig-zagging, and light flashing, my car would be right behind them at the traffic light or toll booth. Bluster doesn't make us faster. Bluster is, well, bluster.

Finally, luck and faith.

Luck is on the list because not everything is in our control. The stoics tell us we can only control our reaction to events, which is an important clue. I don't believe we can make our luck, but we can prepare ourselves when it comes, or be sensitive to its presence.

I say faith because there is much we don't know in terms of both knowledge and the future. The future is unknown and has not been lived yet, and we will never have perfect knowledge because we cannot tell the future. So, faith in ourselves, our abilities, and our hopes and expectations is important and necessary to keep us going.

I believe that if we keep working on our legal skillset, remain patient, humble, and open-minded, cultivate the appropriate friends and comrades-in-arms, take our time, grow organically, be ready for luck, and keep the faith, we will get to wherever we want to be.

That was how I came to answer the question I asked myself.

Coming Around to Conveyancing

When I worked in my father's firm, I generally avoided conveyancing work, that is, sale and purchase transactions of landed property.

However, I would take on a file or two, now and again. I did this to learn and remind myself of the ways in which the process took place. I worked on contracts for selling and purchasing landed properties with titles and those without it, with loans or without, for apartments, houses, or land. No exotic animals or bizarre objects for us, as we lacked the wildly eccentric clients likely to possess such things.

I went back to conveyancing now and again to see if I would take to it. You never know. Sometimes, enjoying something we previously didn't is a matter of timing, context, or incentives. But earlier on, wherever conveyancing was concerned, I did know. Conveyancing was like vegetables when I was young: I disliked it greatly.

It also had too little legal drama and action about it. There is no demand to read urgently, widely, or deeply about the law for the usual sale and purchase transactions. If at all the transaction goes wrong, then sure, we bring out the books. But there is little need to work on the transaction itself. The contracts have seasoned templates that require some revision to customize it for the transaction, the standard forms and letters are set, and the places to submit the relevant documents are known: the stamping office, the land office, the banks, and the other party's solicitors. The application of the law is only prominent in concluding the terms of the agreement; the rest of it is administered to facilitate the transaction.

Dot the i's and cross the t's and do things when they are supposed to be done, and it's all good. That's conveyancing. It's not as if litigation lacks that aspect, but it has its less contentious elements and moments too. Litigation also has its regular Himalayas to cross, dragons to slay, catacombs to discover, and hotel buffets to pillage. So, it has a touch of more drama, urgency, and a whole lot at stake to go with the food, drink, and law.

And there is a lot of law at play. It doesn't begin or end with procedural and substantive law, the easier areas of the field. The challenges that arise when we have to contend with the likes of Murphy's law, Finagle's corollary to Murphy's law, Murphy's Second Corollary, Hofstadter's Law, Parkinson's Law, Willoughby's Law, Monly's Rule, Peter's Principle, Power Law Distribution, Sayre's Law, Goodhart's Law, and so on.

As I said, there are a lot of laws going on.

When I started my firm, I assembled my lawyers and pupils and told them: 'We are a litigation firm. I want us to do kick-ass litigation work and have fun while doing it. I don't care if it's civil, corporate, criminal, industrial, arbitration, or anything else; if there's a dispute to be resolved or fought out, we'll do it and do it well. I don't want us doing anything else. So, no conveyancing, trademark, or administrative kind of work. If you get that kind of work, you are at liberty to reject it.'

A few months after my firm was set up, my maternal uncle called me up.

'Hey Fahri, how's the firm going?'

'Ok lah, Uncle. Taking it one month at a time. So far, so good. What's up?'

'I bought this apartment some time back. Recently, the developer sent me a letter. They are asked me to see their lawyer to sign some document, a memorandum of transfer?'

'Ah. That means the title for your apartment is out.'

'Oh. What does that mean?' he asked.

'That letter is telling you that the title for your apartment has been issued. The developer can now register the property transfer into your name on the title.'

'So, what do I have to do?'

'All you have to do is sign the memorandum of transfer, which we call an MOT. Then, you have to settle the stamp duty and ensure the property assessment is paid up. The developer's lawyers will submit the MOT with the title to the relevant land office. The land office will process the transfer and issue you a copy of the title with your name on it.'

'I see. Can you do it for me?'

It was a simple matter. Even the developer's lawyer could have helped him with it.

But this was my uncle, someone I liked. He looked for me because I am the lawyer for my mom's side of the family. He was always nice to me growing up. He had always invited us to his excellent Chinese New Year and Christmas cookouts, even taking me to play tennis with him when I was younger.

When I put all that together, along with telling him to go somewhere else because I only handled litigation, I felt petty and unhelpful. Wasn't I supposed to help those I could within my capacity? This was my family, moreover, and it wasn't as if I had much to do then either.

I wavered as I recalled my little speech to the troops a few months prior. Doing this little piece of work didn't mean we were now a conveyancing firm. I was wrestling with it in my mind.

'Fahri? You there?'

'Sorry, Uncle. Yes. Yes, I'm here. I spaced out for a moment.'

'Oh, sorry. I know you must be busy. Did you manage to catch what I said earlier?'

'Yes, Uncle. I heard, of course. Of course, we'll sort you out. I'll send you a text to tell you what I need, and we take it from there?'

'Okay. I will wait for it. I am glad you can do it for me. I know you just started out so I don't expect you to do it for free, yah? Please send me your bill. Thanks, Fahri!'

Then and there, I liked him some more.

Several months later, out of the blue, I received a call from a company my father had helped a few years ago. I had previously also worked for them, back when I was at my father's firm, but nothing in a major capacity. The company was my father's client, and he dealt with them mostly. I did, however, get to know the company's founder's children at a few social events and discovered we shared a penchant for dry English humour.

After some small talk, they asked whether I could handle a sale and purchase transaction for them. At the time, I was going through a challenging stretch: I had four lawyers on a learning curve with not enough paid litigation work to go around. So, naturally, I said yes. It was fortunate I did, as that transaction carried the firm for a few months.

I approached the recap of conveyancing practice with a beginner's mind, Lainah Oi Lin Yow's *Conveyancing Practice and Procedure in West Malaysia*, a consideration of a selection of reported cases on lawyer's negligence, and a whole lot of curiosity and humility.

Conveyancing is not too difficult: it's mundane, transactional work. Everyone is always waiting on someone else, and there's not a whole lot to do in between. And yet, it is important that the lawyer gets it right because if they don't, all kinds of things could go wrong.

The part that worried me the most turned out to be the least warranted: presenting the transfer documents at the land office. I had heard all kinds of horror stories about transfer documents being rejected for what I felt were the flimsiest of excuses. I wanted to avoid that. So, prior to the actual presentation, I went to the land office to learn how it was done.

It was not very different from what my father had made do during my pupillage. He wanted me to learn things from the ground up, so he did not allow me to use the office dispatch initially. I was made to do everything myself: I did service of documents, affidavits of service, affirmed it, company and IC searches, photocopying, bundling, and filing. The first few affidavits were my affidavits of service.

'If you do it yourself, you know what it takes and how long it takes to get done. When you know, the clerks and dispatch boys cannot fool you,' he had said.

Big truth in that.

I arrived at the land office in black and white clothes. The officer at the inquiry counter looked at me with bemusement and asked me what I was doing there. I told him I had just established my firm and had a conveyancing file to handle. Since I had no clerk or dispatch to help me, I had to learn how to do it myself until I could afford one. I also asked him if he would he be kind enough to help me.

And that opened up a new world of help.

The officer broke into a smile and immediately got down to patiently explaining the process and what I needed to do to ensure the documents presented were not rejected. After the briefing, he gave me a file to put all the documents together for presentation. He even wrote down the list of what needed to be presented on a scrap of paper and put it in the envelope.

I thanked him profusely for his kindness and instructions. He said lawyers were uncommon at the land office, as mostly runners or public members handled the transaction on their own. Moreover, the lawyers who turned up were often arrogant and disrespectful. He remarked that I was unusual in forthrightly declaring my ignorance.

That day, I left the land office very pleased, thinking what a beautiful world we would all live in if we were a little more helpful to each other like that.

The conveyancing work that had unexpectedly fallen into my lap allowed me to reacquaint myself with it. While I found enjoyment in my own way in such work, I did not see myself doing this either solely or daily. Being a supervisory role for such a work suffices because it does not often require sustained and intense scrutiny like a litigation case, unless something goes wrong or there is some complexity to the transaction.

When I returned to the land office to present the transfer documents for registration, I met the same officer who had checked my document folder to ensure everything was in order. It was presented and accepted without any incident.

I went on to do a few more sale and purchase transactions on my own because none of my lawyers were interested in touching it and would rather do a trial! As much as I was annoyed about it, I completely empathized, for I had been like them before.

Even though our first year started with, 'I'm sorry, we do only litigation work', the next year, we were in a different zone, that of, 'Of course, we do sale and purchase transactions! What type of property is it and is this with title or without?'

How Litigation Experience Helps Contract Drafting

My father stopped going to court in 1988. Save for moving or attending calls to the Bar[33], or giving evidence at trial, he avoided the visits. He was a 'corporate lawyer'.

A corporate lawyer prefers the boardrooms to the courts, as their practice is focused entirely on contractual and corporate advisory matters. They prowl boardrooms, general meetings, and hotel conference rooms, while litigators prowl the courts, tribunals, and police stations. I knew a corporate lawyer who was so averse to courts that he could not even attend his pupil's call, purportedly because he was so nervous about being in court.

When I was in his firm, my father had a rule: If I wanted to be a corporate lawyer, I would first have to spend a few years in litigation. He felt those initial litigation years would inculcate good habits and provide for a well-rounded education to be a corporate lawyer.

First, as litigators, we always have to be on top of the law. We need to know the latest decisions and how they fit with previous court decisions. Knowing the latest cases and law gives us a competitive advantage over those who are

[33] An occasion when a person is admitted and enrolled as an advocate and solicitor on the High Court roll.

lackadaisical about their reading, and their numbers are legion. A good litigator makes it a point to know and understand the latest legal developments.

A corporate lawyer with litigation grounding is likelier to form a habit of regularly reading decided cases. My father often complained that the corporate lawyers he dealt with didn't know or bother to catch up on the latest verdicts. If we were unfamiliar with a certain latest Federal Court decision, which impacted a contract we were drafting for a client, our ignorance would leave us open to a claim for negligence.

Secondly, and related to reading cases, a corporate lawyer should know how a contract can go wrong, and think about suitable clauses or wordings to avoid such a situation. Often, corporate lawyers draft contracts and go on their merry way afterwards. They are usually not around, in fact long gone, when there is a dispute. That's when the litigators come in.

In the early 2000s, I handled claims for a nursing college against nurses and their guarantor parents or relatives for breach of scholarship contracts. The scholarships varied from RM 30,000 to RM 40,000 in value, depending on where they went to study nursing. In exchange, they would be bonded to the nursing college for at least five years after graduation and could be posted to any hospital with which the nursing college had a tie-up.

I was busy with such cases because, at the time, there was a huge demand for nurses in Dubai. Nurses could earn ten to fifteen times more than they would in Malaysia. As a result, many breached their scholarships to fly to Dubai, and it made sense. They would have earned more than enough to pay off the scholarship after half a year's salary.

Now, you would think the claims were a sure-fire winner, no-look slam-dunk win, and you would be right. Except that if you were the other side's lawyer and diligently read the scholarship agreement, you should have encountered an arbitration clause close to the end of the contract. If you were sharp enough, you would have applied to refer the claim for arbitration under the then in-force Section 6 of the Arbitration Act 1952 and jammed my claim in the courts.

That happened, but thankfully, it wasn't a regular objection. Even though I could and would defeat the application, it slowed the claim's progress and added cost.

In any event, it was silly to have an arbitration clause for a low-value scholarship claim. We usually refer matters to arbitration when they involve a high degree of technical expertise, where the parties want privacy, or when the claims are of great value and immense complexity, *not* a RM 40,000 claim for a breach of a scholarship agreement.

I called the group legal manager to ask her why there was an arbitration clause in the scholarship agreement. She responded that it was part of the 'usual boilerplate clauses at the back of the contract'. I advised them to revise their contracts to eliminate the clause immediately, and they eventually did.

If she had understood the litigation dimension in the presence of such a clause, she would not have allowed it to be part of the terms. Exposing contractual terms to litigation will test a contract's mettle. It is in litigation that we discover the many ways a contract is deficient and realize the clauses that have more than a significant influence on the course of litigation. Learning from those experiences better informs our clause selection and clause drafting.

Third, by handling contractual dispute claims, we experience what goes into such a dispute, while we engage with it at a working level. It is from our first-hand working experience that we gain a deeper insight into the process of crafting better terms that improve the operational aspects of litigation for effectiveness and success.

Here is an example. Order 10, Rule 3 of the Rules of Court 2012 (RC2012)[34] recognizes that if a term in a contract specifies how the service of a document is to be carried out, that term will regulate the service of documents between the parties. This means that we can include a term in the contract to specify how or where the service will take place.

If we were corporate lawyers drafting a contract and had some litigation experience, we would have the insight to craft a service of documents clause to serve the Writ of Summons or Originating Summons by way of e-mail or WhatsApp in the event legal proceedings had to be initiated. Such a clause cuts down the time, effort, and cost of service and the challenges in personally serving the claim on the other party if a litigation dispute should break out. It's a small but significant thing when the dispute hits the courts.

It is an example of how litigation experience can inform and improve the contract drafting and thinking experience. An experienced litigator will advise against including an arbitration clause in a scholarship contract.

This is how that experience can influence and shape the contractual terms in a contract.

Finally, a litigator's drafting is more likely to be more cogent and to the point than a corporate lawyer's drafting—in theory, of course. This generalization applies to the mediocre ones, and there is little qualitative difference between a top litigator and a top corporate lawyer.

---

[34] Rules of Court, 2012 - The Malaysian Bar (2012) The Malaysian Bar. Available at: https://www.malaysianbar.org.my/document/com_docman/gid/itemid&rid=18971 (Accessed: 16 December 2024).

A litigator drafts and crafts documents principally for the court's consumption. Yes, it is also for the opposite side, but they are not the priority. The court is busy—constantly, perpetually, and relentlessly busy. In writing for the courts, litigators have to balance cogency, thoroughness, and conciseness for busy people who need to quickly absorb and manage large amounts of complex and complicated information in order to come to a decision. This is a litigator's audience, and, therefore, the writing has to be simple, and the content distilled and precise while respecting the complexity of the matter.

A corporate lawyer should write similarly, and I am not suggesting they don't. However, they don't have to because they write for a different audience. Conciseness is less of an issue because the audience is interested more in getting their money's worth from the lawyers and the deal they were hired for. The audience, on the other hand, is more concerned about completeness than conciseness—or at least the appearance of it.

Having said that, it does not mean that a corporate lawyer who does not go through litigation is any lesser. I know excellent corporate lawyers who have no litigation experience. It is essentially about the quantity and quality of experience and what we do with it.

It also means that a corporate lawyer's experience has room for a wider and greater depth of diversity, more opportunities to learn from different domains, and a richer professional experience. While it works, its opposite is true as well. A litigator who has meaningful experience in corporate legal work will enjoy the same benefits, advantages, and awareness from such an opportunity.

Whatever the case, I cannot see how one loses out on having experience of another area of law.

Being a Commissioner for Oaths and a Notary Public

When I was young, I was greatly impressed by my father signing things.

There was a sense of importance and occasion to whatever he put his signature to. He always looked serious whenever he did so. I saw him sign many things: documents, forms of various shapes and sizes, cheques, credit card slips, registers—all sorts.

Every time he signed anything, something new would emerge: I got a new computer or we stayed at a hotel, or new furniture arrived at the house or there was a new car in the driveway or someone came to visit us. People seemed to want his signature. He seemed important because his personal handwritten mark was required.

Back then, to me, that whole signing thing was a kind of magic. There was power in his signature. As a child, I would hope that one day I would get the opportunity to sign some things or make my signature important enough to be on a piece of paper. It's funny how life works out.

I started signing things on a regular basis after I started working. Despite the delight and pleasure of signing off on letters for the firm on my own and imprinting my unique signature on documents, the novelty wore off quickly. By then, for work, I had to sign letters, vouchers, court lists and slips, my own affidavits, and the like. There was something to sign a few times each day.

I first got into heavy-duty signing when I was made the secretary of the KL LAC, for a while. Back then, it was located at the now-demolished Wisma Kraftangan near the Masjid Jamek LRT station on Jalan Tun Perak. I was elected as a result of actively contributing at the KL LAC at the time.

My first encounter with it was when, one day, in my first month as the secretary, I was led into a small room next to the head of the KL LAC's room. Inside, there was a table with two chairs. On the table were two neat thick stacks of papers, which looked intimidating. They seemed like twin pillars standing together in defiance against chaos. In front of the table were two chairs.

'What am I supposed to do?' I asked.

'These are the thank you letters to the LAC volunteers,' replied the staff or officer who drew me there.

'That's a lot.'

'Yeah. We have a backlog. Thank you for signing them.'

I sat and signed for the next twenty minutes or so—one letter after the other.

I signed them all earnestly, making sure that it didn't look casual or careless. I wanted the signature to impress not just visually on paper, but the volunteers too with its contents that were deliberate, mindful, and above all, heartfelt from the KL LAC to them. If you were a volunteer who received one of those letters and felt the back of it, where my signature was, you could trace the imprint of it. That's the KL LAC passion I was trying to transmit.

But that was expecting too much from the volunteer recipient.

One day, while signing, of course, I happened to ask myself what I would do if I received one of these letters. An image of me glancing at the letter and binning or filing it immediately came as a response. It was entirely true, of course. Both are the same because even though I file things, I may as well bin them. After all, eventually, I don't know where I put them.

With that realization, my life's 'signing in earnest' phase drew to a close.

From then on, I was a signature machine. I could blaze through a pile of 'thank you', 'how do you do' and whatchamacallits quicker and quicker, until we cleared the backlog and were on top of our correspondence. If there were an international legal aid letter signing competition back then, I feel sure I would be in the top ten. Okay lah, top five. But yes, I was fast.

When I was signing intensely, I had a flow. After establishing a rhythm in the first few letters, I merged with the moment, and everything segued into a flurry of paper and hand movements. It was only after I finished the last piece that I felt the weariness in my right hand and wrist.

In a civilized society, we have to sign for things. The older I grew, the more I had to sign professionally and personally—and regularly, too. If I wanted things done, if I didn't want them done; if I wanted in, if I wanted out—everything required a signature. I couldn't get out of it even if I wanted to. I did not have a choice in the matter anymore.

But that is changing—in a way. PINs, passwords, patterns, facial IDs, and fingerprints are now the most common ways we verify ourselves. We now use computers and phones more to transact than paper. The relentless efficiency of assigned code irons out another quirk of human behaviour.

As more legal transactions are done through computers and online, there will be less of a need for a physical signature. There will be some digital verification tokens, or DTV, that will be unique to us. There will no longer be any biological feature of us in that DTV. Once technologies that facilitate forgeries and fakery are low cost and prevalent (as I feel they are now) and biometric verification (or whatever technology) becomes cheap, accessible, and a practical substitute, it will be the end of signatures, which will eventually become a curiosity in the future. 'So that's how people in the old days showed tangible consent!'

As an adult, that power my father wielded whenever he signed something in my childhood now seemed more like a shackle than a spear. I was chained to signing for things. While it may now be digitized, it is no less real and insistent.

In my twelfth year of practice, I decided if I was still going to sign all this stuff, I'd like to be paid it, and have a fancy title to go along with it. So, I applied to be a Commissioner for Oaths, or CFO.

I thought I'd just try it on for size and see what it was like. I confess I liked the title of 'Commissioner': It sounded grand, even if it was only related to oaths. I applied with the Chief Registrar of the Federal Court's Office in 2011 and received my appointment in 2012. Back then, its tenure was a year and renewals had to happen accordingly. I renewed it only once. Before 2018, given the miserly fees we could charge, being a CFO did not seem worthy of a lawyer's time or effort.

I remember once, in my first year as a CFO, spending half-an-hour with a lady who insisted I attest her signature on a blank piece of paper and certify a true copy of documents for which she did not bring the originals. She claimed that government officials had insisted on it, but I politely declined regardless. Unfortunately, she insisted so strongly that I had to revoke her occupancy licence and threatened to take action against her for trespass before she left.

Incidents like these helped me understand why CFOs I often met were wary, dismissive, and grumpy. Their job is perfunctory, the fee apittance, and whenever the clientele is unreasonable or bizarre, it can be off-putting, even if it happens occasionally.

Much of the trouble lies in the fact that few understand the role of a CFO. Aside from 'chopping and signing', the public does not know what they can or cannot do. The same could be said for some CFOs, too. Their work relates primarily to the attestation of signatures and swearing of oaths. A CFO's signature is a consequence and a confirmation that the attestation process was complied with and the document was sworn before them.

Another notable incident in my first year was when a well-known young Malay actor dropped into my father's office to have an *afidavit bujang*[35] done, a document verifies the deponent is unmarried—a compulsion for Malaysian Muslims for their application to marry. I had no idea who that actor was, but the female staff in my father's office were in a flutter. I heard them through my door but dismissed it as some heated gossip that broke out every now and again.

After a short while, my door inched open. The receptionist's head emerged eventually, and asked, with extra and unusual politeness, if I could go down now and attend to someone who needed CFO services.

As I headed downstairs, I saw the female staff look at me expectantly. It was eerie and weirded me out. I turned to them at the top of the stairs and asked, 'What's wrong with all of you

[35] An affidavit verifying the deponent was not currently married and single.

today? Is it something about the guy downstairs?' They turned coy and looked down sheepishly.

It was a pupil in a *tudung labuh* who said breathlessly, 'Oh Encik Fahri, it's [I forgot his name]. He acted in [so and so movie]. He is a famous actor. He's very handsome! Oh my god! I can't believe he is downstairs!' And they all got wound up again.

I saw the actor on the ground floor. The receptionist sat him down at my CFO table behind my mother's beautiful black lacquered vintage six-panelled Chinese screen embedded with jade and mother-of-pearl inlays.

I introduced myself. It was difficult to ignore his good looks.

'So, I hear you are a famous actor.' I said.

'It would not seem so,' he replied.

'Oh, why is that?'

'Well, if you don't know who I am, how can I be famous?'

We both laughed. He was witty and handsome. Bastard.

'So, what can I do for you today?'

'I need an affidavit bujang? They said I was supposed to see a CFO about it.'

'I see. Do you have the affidavit? Or do you need one drafted?'

'No. Can you draft it for me?'

'Sure.'

'Alright. Let's do it.'

I took his identity card and went upstairs. When I got to the top, the ladies gathered to hear my report about him.

'So, what did you think of him, Encik Fahri?'

'Well, ladies. He is very handsome and humble. I am happy to report he is witty too.'

'Tu lah, we heard you laughing with him, Sir!' exclaimed the tudung labuh pupil excitedly.

'Ha? Well, I am sorry to disappoint you ladies. He requested that I prepare him an afidavit bujang. So, if you will excuse me, I must not detain this man any longer than is necessary.'

The room fell into lamentation and sighs. I scurried to the safety of my room to prepare his affidavit.

Previously, statutory declarations and court affidavits were four ringgit per attestation for the original copy and two ringgits for each duplicate copy of an affidavit. If there are exhibits, it costs two ringgits for each in the original affidavit and one ringgit per exhibit for each copy.

In my first two years as a CFO, I spent more on my chops, signage, name tag, and register than what I collected from my service. My takings were measly. I attribute it to my insistence that the deponents attend before me at my office for it to be done. There are CFOs who agree to witness your signature without you signing or appearing before them. I call those attestations in absentia requests. I don't practice them, for it's wrong, of course; but those who do, tend to charge a premium for that privilege.

In 2018, the fee for attesting court affidavits was increased. It is now ten ringgit per attestation for the original copy and five ringgits for each duplicate copy. Now, it is five ringgit per exhibit for the original affidavit and two ringgit per exhibit for the affidavit copy. These days, there is less of a need for duplicates because most documents are converted to PDF format, from which copies can be made. At the most, many just have a duplicate made. The days of 'need to prepare several copies for a court document' are over.

For my firm, I rarely attest court affidavits. Most of my attestations are statutory declarations (SDs), then and now. I estimate that 90 per cent of my work as a CFO is statutory declaration attestations.

In 2016, however, the Chief Registrar's Office changed the CFO application process, making it more onerous for applicants. This was an attempt to raise the standards of those appointed CFOs. The sentiment was laudable, but the execution left room for improvement.

Instead of simply filling out an application, we had to sit for an exam and an interview. There were several questions: I forget how many—fifty, sixty, or something like that, which had to be answered in an hour-and-a-half. I remember being told vividly that we could not get more than seven questions wrong, crossing which would result in a failure. I wasn't so worried about the law, as the CFO rules were straightforward and few. However, I was concerned about the general section of the paper, wherein, they could ask us just about anything, and there were ten questions to attend to.

Boy, they did ask us *anything*.

A question I particularly remember getting wrong was about the tallest building in Asia. I recall sitting in the exam hall, thinking, 'What has this question got to do with anything I have to do as a CFO?'

Of course, I thought so only because I didn't know the answer. My guess was Shanghai Tower. When I checked it right after the exam, I found that it was wrong. The correct answer is the Burj Khalifa. If you didn't know that, now you do. Congratulations.

All in all, I reckoned I got six questions wrong. My calculations were confirmed when the results were sent to us via email. I had passed the exam.

Since they didn't send us individual results, but an overall score list of lawyer and public member candidates, I could not help but look.

It was brutal.

The passing rate on the public members' list was about 10 per cent. For lawyers, it was about 30 per cent, something I felt was disappointing, since *we* are lawyers and, therefore, we are supposed to be adept at law. Yes, the questions were tricky, but not difficult. Spending time understanding what they ask of us pays dividends when we eventually get down to writing our answer. As for the general questions, I have no idea how to prepare for them.

I thought the interviews were merely a formality, just like they were before. But not this time. We were asked questions that tested our knowledge of the rules. We had to justify why our appointment would be good for our area. Thankfully, that query was easy for me: There was no CFO in Mutiara Damansara, where my firm was located. The areas around us—Damansara Perdana, Kota Damansara, Bandar Utama and Taman Tun Dr Ismail—had one, but ours didn't.

Why am I still a CFO, despite arguing that the fee is not worth the time for a lawyer, that CFO attestations should be abolished, and that signatures—and, by implication, the CFO's role in attesting them—are unnecessary?

One, because the law still requires it. Two, it has a demand. Three, I have been told directly, and my clerks have confirmed it too, that many find our location convenient. Four, we charge reasonably.

I have had some clients who were shocked when I informed them our prices, while some even claimed that other CFOs charge from twenty to fifty ringgit per attestation. 'If I could charge more, I would; but I can't,' I have often told them.

However, we tend to get those people's friends and family afterwards. So, while we lose out by not conning others, we make up for it with referrals.

Let's face it: If we wanted to cheat and overcharge those who came to us, we could. But I am not comfortable with earning money unfairly, nor do I have any interest in dealing with the consequences of such conduct.

Finally, and above all, even though it is an inconvenience to us and not a 'profit-making' endeavour, it remains a service to the community. It may be minor, but it can become crucial and urgent for some. Whenever I hear good feedback from clients or read positive reviews online, I am assured this service benefits others, something which is a personal pleasure to me—a little bit of the sense of service over self.

I am also a Notary Public (NP).

Only lawyers with fifteen years in practice can apply to be NPs. In 2015, after I completed fifteen years at the Bar, I thought of trying it out.

An application to be a Notary Public is made to the Attorney General's Chambers (AGC) online at the AGC portal. This is a simpler process compared to a CFO application, as there are no exams or interviews. Requirements include submission of the required documents, payment of the application fee of RM 1,000 for a two-year appointment, and our patience as the AGC goes around collecting letters of no objections to our appointment.

If all goes well, our application is approved, and we receive the physical copy of our appointment certificate.

From my experience, being an NP is far, far, far more worthwhile compared to a CFO.

For one, far fewer duties are assigned to us as NPs because we are already bound by our ethical conduct as lawyers. Thus, we are less regulated about how we carry out our work.

Secondly, the fee for attestations is higher than what CFOs can charge, even with the 2018 revision. For example, NPs can charge twenty-five ringgit per attestation for the original and half that for the copy. CFOs can charge only ten ringgit per attestation. There is a fifteen-ringgit difference between the attestation fee of an NP and CFO.

Thirdly, lawyers don't have to spend money on anything to reflect our NP status, except a change in the letterhead and perhaps the website. CFOs, however, have to put up a signboard stating the fees they are entitled to charge, along with another one that states their powers. CFOs have to also display their instrument of appointment and, thus, must wear a name tag while working. If you ask me, I only think I look cool wearing a name tag if I have a cowboy hat on, am decked out in full cowboy garb, and am sitting on a large, powerful horse named Daisy, with the reins in my left hand and a loaded shotgun in my right.

Fourthly, and most importantly, I recovered my NP expenses in three months, while I took far longer to recover my CFO expenses.

Despite that, NP fees are in desperate need of revision. They are regulated by the Notaries Public (Fees) (No. 1) Rules 1981 (published as PU(A) 198/81)[36], and have been drafted by the Rules Committee. They came into force on 1 August 1981, more than thirty years ago.

Fifthly, NPs have the privilege of certifying document copies as genuine. The only other legally authorized person who can do that is an advocate and solicitor. CFOs cannot do this.

[36] Fees (2021) Notary Public Malaysia. Available at: https://www.notarypublicmalaysia.com/fees/#:~:text=A%20notary%20public%20may%20charge%20fees%20as%20provided (Accessed: 16 December 2024).

There is a grave and prevalent misconception that CFOs can certify copies of documents. They cannot, as they are not authorized to. Yet, even government departments demand that document copies be certified by CFOs. Whenever I complained about them to the Chief Registrar's Office, requesting them to educate the relevant government department, nothing happened.

Certifying copies of documents as genuine comprises most of our NP work, and this is where the heaviest number of signings happen. To CTC something is to Certify True-Copy of a document. Some clients have us CTC every page of a passport copy or a lengthy agreement, and have large amounts of documents to CTC in one go.

NP work can be lucrative, but that's only in relation to CFO work. We cannot depend on it to fuel the office with its lawyers and staff. On a very good day, and those are uncommon, it can take care of the petty cash for the month—and that's as far as it goes. All things considered, it earns us far less money than our regular litigation and corporate work.

The reasons I gave for being a CFO, despite the downsides, are the same ones as that of being an NP: To provide a service to the community nearby and adjacent that needs them. As a CFO, NP, and advocate and solicitor (A&S), I can advise those who come by on what the difference is and which is most appropriate to a client's purpose.

This can be summarized as follows: CFOs are for domestic documents that require attestation. A&S can also CTC domestic documents. NPs, however, are for documents used internationally, and there, they can attest affidavits and CTC documents. Interestingly, Sabah and Sarawak lawyers prefer their signatories to sign before NPs instead of CFOs.

I feel our CFO/NP services have a tiny positive spillover effect on the other businesses, particularly the restaurants nearby. Often, while the clients wait for their appointment or after they finish their appointment, they stop by the mamak or one of the favoured restaurants nearby.

The other reason why I enjoy providing that service is the people I get to meet. When I have the time, I like chatting and making small talk with the customers. It reminds me that many people are doing various things and leading different, interesting lives. However, that happens only if there's time and opportunity. Most of the time, it's transactional.

Should you take it up? I would not recommend being a CFO, unless you are looking for serendipity and experience, or want to serve the community. There is little money to speak of. Our service is thoroughly and completely unappreciated. We conduct a function no one takes seriously, and we could be doing something more profitable with our time.

It is time to review the need for such a role.

As far as NPs are concerned, I think there is still a need for them, because of the international dimension and reliance placed by parties worldwide on a certified document. For Malaysian lawyers who have been in the game for fifteen years and up, I encourage you to take it up. The more NPs there are, the easier for the public to access such services. The need for it springs eternally.

I will conclude this passage with an incident I once had as an NP, so you have an idea of what I have to put up with occasionally.

I was once asked to notarize some declarations and affidavits for a family, and CTC a slew of family documents. There were not many attestations—maybe four for each family member, who were applying for permanent residency in a European country. The wife and children came and executed the documents.

The husband, however, could not make it. He was African, and overseas. Looking at his stern face in the photocopy of his passport, he looked like someone who would insist I attested 'in absentia'.

And sure enough, he did.

He put a lot of pressure on the agent to have me sign off the pre-signed forms he had sent over. His agent was caught between us, so I decided to spare the poor fellow and resolve the deadlock by speaking to him directly.

'Mr Fahri. Why you make things so difficult? I sent you my whole family to do our documents with you. I paid a lot of money to have them with your signature. My family, they all vouch that I signed it. I am now in Europe. I am coming back only next week. Can you just please just sign my documents? My agent needs to submit it soon.'

'I hear you, Mr Difficult. I have clarified it with your agent. You have time when you get back. Don't worry about it. Once you arrive in Malaysia, he will arrange for it. We have time.'

'Come on, Mr Fahri. This is not good service. You are making it difficult for me. I signed the documents, and now, I assure you on the phone about the same. Is it still not good enough? This is ridiculous. There is no dispute I signed it.'

'Mr Difficult, please. You are misunderstanding. It has nothing to do with my trust of you. My job is to ensure two things: one, that you are who you say you are; two, making sure you sign it in front of me. Then, I put my own signature to confirm you did both of these things. If I don't comply with this procedure, then I haven't done my job. That's all. It has nothing to do with trusting you, Mr Difficult.'

'You can still do your job if you take my word for it. Your job is to make sure it is me, I, Mr Difficult, who signs it. Now I'm telling you it's me, and I have signed it. Are you saying you don't trust me, Mr Fahri? You just met my family, my wife, my children. My agent can verify my identity. I have also paid your fees. How is it you don't trust me?'

Not bad, I thought. He could have done a little better with the argument.

'It's not a lack of trust, Mr Difficult. Okay, like this lah. Since you are insistent, I am prepared to consider doing it for five thousand ringgit per signature.'

'WHAT?! This is ridiculous! You are unreasonable, Mr Fahri! Twenty thousand only for four signatures?! You are trying to rob me!'

'No, Mr Difficult. I am not. We charge twenty-five ringgit per attestation. But you have to do it at my office. I want you here, in my office. Let me make it clear: I don't want your five thousand; I prefer the twenty-five ringgits. I want you in front of me. That's all. You are the one hassling me to breach my legal duty.'

He went quiet for a few moments.

'Fine. I will see you when I get back.'

And he did. He signed his declarations and affidavits before me for the usual fee. We both went our ways with our respective peace of mind intact.

My Journey to the Syariah Bar

I was finally called to the Syariah (Federal Territories) Bar in June 2018.

On my fifth attempt.

The journey started in 2010 when I had signed up for the Post Graduate Diploma in Syariah and Practice (DSP) in Universiti Teknologi MARA (UiTM). I did the course with Syahrul Syazwan, my pupil at the time, and his housemate, Azwar. They both had recently graduated from UiTM. I did it to have the DSP as my course content for the Kuala Lumpur Syariah Bar exam I intended to take. It was also meant to be my second encounter with the Syariah or Islamic law; I had taken it as an elective subject in my final year at Bristol University.

The DSP course was held every Saturday. It ran from eight in the morning to nine at night, for nine months. Every Saturday, we had two-hour lectures on each subject, one after the other, breaking only for lunch from one to two in the afternoon. This was followed by more two-hour lectures, one after the other, until nine at night. Despite all those hours, many of us did not pay attention. The study material was tedious, and the lecturers were tedium.

Our bodies may have been present, but our minds were elsewhere. I felt like I was back in secondary school, but now, as a grown-up lawyer with a family. Most of us were on Facebook, watching movies with subtitles, texting, or doing other work, rather than paying attention. Syahrul, Azwar, and I saw everything from our seats at the back-middle of the class, where I was busy writing essays for Loyarburok. It was a delight to discover I was at my creative and productive height when I should have rather been focused on the lecture.

There was a ten to fifteen minute interval at the end of each lecture. Not that it was scheduled, but because we needed a cigarette break from pretending to pay attention.

Duplicity is tiring.

I don't know how anyone can learn anything like that—hour after hour of lectures, like waves crashing upon an indifferent boulder. But it seems to be a Malaysian education thing. I received the same treatment for my Certificate of Legal Practice course in 1998. We had several different law lectures scheduled back-to-back over several hours. Although my mind would switch off after forty-five minutes, my hand continued writhing like a leopard gecko's tail after it fell off. My right hand worked directly with my eyes and ears, bypassing my mind, recording for posterity.

Sometimes, when the lecturers could not make it as per schedule, they would schedule a three-hour lecture extravaganza to compensate. And if two of them wanted to reschedule, we would have those epic, five or six-hours-long lectures.

This was vastly different from our university lectures in England, where the duration of a lecture was an hour, at the maximum. The lecturers were often done by the fiftieth, or latest by the fifty-fifth minute. Then, they left us alone with our reading list. It was rare for the faculty to fix one lecture immediately after another. If it happened, it was usually because of the electives we took. Law undergraduates were given plenty of time and space to read, explore, think, and reflect. The theory that went around was that the law course at Bristol had the second-least lecture hours; English literature was one below us.

My sense of it is that Malaysian 'educators' see their students as empty vessels. Since the endeavour of education is simply a matter of filling an empty thing up, our time is meant to be spent acquiring information, and then tested for retention through exams. Poor results mean poor absorption of information, while good results reflect a mind that knows what to regurgitate on cue. This 'filling empty vessels' mindset conceives scheduling law lectures (or any subject) back-to-back for long hours. In all that yammering, learning is lost, and understanding remains primordial.

A week before the final exams for the DSP, our *usul fiqh*[37] lecturer called me out of the blue.

'The exam starts next week. How is your preparation?' he asked.

'It is good, *uztad. Insyallah*, I should be prepared for it.'

'Good. Good. I called you because I want you to consider wearing a *songkok* for the exams.'

'I see. If that is the case, of course, I will wear it. I didn't know it was compulsory.'

'No, no. It's not compulsory. I am worried they will stop you from entering the hall, if you are not appropriately dressed.

'I see. May I ask, what is the songkok supposed to do?'

'To tuck your hair under, of course! Yours is long. An examiner may object to you entering the hall. You should wear a songkok and tuck your hair under it. That's what I wanted to suggest to you.'

---

[37] Islamic jurisprudence

'I see. I see. Thank you for your advice, uztad. I will take it.'

On the first day of the exam, as I walked towards the hall, everyone saw me wearing the songkok. I drew curious looks, amused smiles, and discrete finger-pointing. I could not have stood out more if I had taken my pants off. They all had a look about them which asked, *Why is he wearing that for the exam? Has he got some kind of trick going on?*

When I reached the examination hall, where Syahrul was, I was pleased. Turns out he was the only other guy wearing one, for he, too, had long hair. We were, of course, teased by our amused classmates. *The songkok will not buy you marks, lah! That's not the way to win Allah's favour. Maybe after this, they will become the uztads instead. What hypocrites!* the glares seemed to say.

I eventually passed all my exams and graduated on 25 November 2010, together with Syahrul and Azwar.

In 2011, I signed up to take the Kuala Lumpur Syariah Bar exams right after that.

How we went about it back then, until 2016, was that we first attended a day of lectures, which were from nine in the morning to five in the evening. The allotted time for each lecturer was an hour-and-a-half. You could only cram four lectures of that duration in a day. They would often comprise picking four subjects: Syariah criminal procedure, Syariah civil procedure, Islamic family law, the Islamic administration, and its organizations or a lecture about relevant civil court decisions that involve the Syariah courts or the state religious department.

We were lectured on four subjects but tested on six. The latter included *usul fiqh*, *Fara'id*[38] formulas and calculations, translating a scholar's text from Arabic to Malay, Syariah evidence, civil and criminal procedure, and family and criminal

[38] Islamic inheritance

law. Unless you could read or write Arabic, you would be deprived of one compulsory question, as I was. I burned ten marks, skipping the translation question on top of another five for not attending all the classes.

After a day of lectures, we sat for the exam the next day.

There were no courses or textbooks you could rely on for the exam, no past-year papers to practice, and the *Jurnal Hukum*[39] was not easily accessible, not that it was terribly relevant. Many of us were dependent on 'tips' hinted at by the lecturers about what we could expect for the exam. I felt like I was back in secondary school, sitting for SPM[40] again. Tip. Tip.

Before my first attempt, I had no idea what areas we would be tested on. During the lectures, I heard we would be tested on more or less what I learned for the DSP. But we didn't know what exactly we would be tested on, and how we were expected to answer the questions.

Naturally, I flunked the first time, DSP notwithstanding.

We are not informed of our marks. We are only told whether we passed or failed an exam. Neither do we get to learn from where we went wrong. The question paper is also not allowed to be kept. Nothing is available for reference, study, or practice.

All I knew was I failed. It was frustrating.

For those reasons, I flunked for the second time in 2012 and the third in 2014. It was hard to motivate myself for future exams at the time. There was not enough time and material to process the lectures sufficiently to answer the questions. It was difficult when the exam came right after the lectures. I had to

---

[39] Malaysian journal that reports on only Syariah cases.

[40] Sijil Pelajaran Malaysia or Malaysian Certificate of Education. It is the equivalent of a high school certificate.

do most of the reading and understanding before the lectures, and yet, it did not instil any confidence in me.

In 2017, I picked up new wind and persuaded two of my lawyers, Aizat and Farhan, to sit for the Syariah Bar exams with me. Misery adores company—the more, the merrier. For that year, the exam organizers did something different. We still had a day's lecture, but this time, the exam was held a week later, something I thought was thoughtful and reasonable of them. This time, the tips the lecturers dropped proved to be useful. We had the time to read up and knew our focus areas better.

And yet, Aizat and I failed, but Farhan passed. To me, this felt like an impressive feat, as he was a first-timer who hadn't even taken the DSP! We were happy for him. Aizat, though, was crestfallen.

I was keen to take the exams again after they changed the format to a more reasonable one. Aizat was dissuaded at first, as he was not used to failing. I assured him that not passing was fine so long as we learned from it. His first time was my fourth time, 'So don't take it too hard!' I told him.

I was going to keep at it until I passed. I would sit for the exam until they passed me out of pity! Aizat laughed at that, and agreed to give it another go.

We enrolled for the 2018 exams. Aizat declared that if he failed, he would not reappear for the exam. I wondered how many more times I would have to take it before I passed.

The 2018 exam was a planet-aligned moment. Alhamdulillah, we passed. It was the exam I felt most confident about, compared to the previous four attempts. Aizat and I were called to the Federal Territories Bar on 28 June 2018. I was pleased and proud about finally having the right of audience in the Syariah courts. I could finally get the direct experience of Syariah practice, instead of hearing it from others.

I had never thought I would end up as one and certainly possessed no ambition when I began my legal practice as an advocate and solicitor. However, as the years grew by, I felt there was a need for it, since I was often referred to Syariah's work but could not take it up. Now, I could. I was also curious about what the advocacy was like in the Syariah court and what matters I would get to do as a Syariah practitioner.

In closing, I want to share some advice for Muslim lawyers, something I also tell my non-Muslim lawyers, pupils, and interns. I know it is 'off the shelf' advice—the type I spray about indiscriminately—and it is not tailored to your uniqueness. Think about it and see how it sits with you, before rolling with it or ignoring it.

I encourage you to qualify as a Syariah lawyer in whatever state you are, for it will add value to your practice. It does not necessarily mean you must do family, Syariah criminal defence, estate planning, and advisory work. It is enough that you are qualified and licensed to practice as one.

When I started, I thought this is all there is to it. Since then, I have been appointed to provide expert evidence, legal opinions, contract advisory, and even corporate advisory and compliance work related to Syariah law—the last two being the surprise elements. The work has been more varied and interesting than I had expected, and I look forward to being continually pleasantly surprised.

Having a Syariah certificate of practice allows you and your firm to offer a wider range of services. At the very least, it will bring you a heightened awareness of Syariah issues that may strike matters under your care. I have since found the Syariah to be a fascinating, fertile field of study, discussion, and work.

In my short time at the Syariah Bar, I have formed a tentative view about what a Syariah litigator needs to possess to be considered competent in terms of legal knowledge.

Firstly, they should understand the Federal Constitution, particularly the articles related to the State's power to make Syariah law and the Syariah court's jurisdiction. Since the Syariah courts have an exclusive and limited jurisdiction, it is important to know where those limits lie.

Second, they should be familiar with related legislation that provides the civil court framework.

This would include Part IX of the Federal Constitution, the Courts of Judicature Act 1964, the Subordinate Courts Act 1948, the Civil Law Act 1956, the Interpretations Act 1948 and 1967, and the leading civil cases related to them. Knowing only Syariah law is not enough, a good grasp of common law with all its civil, criminal, and administrative aspects is important and would inform Syariah's practice.

Third, they should know the court practice directions and the legislation enacted that comprises the Syariah law, such as The Administration of Islamic Law (Federal Territory) 1993 (Act 505), the Syariah Court Civil Procedure (Federal Territory) Act 1998 (Act 585), the Islamic Family Law (Federal Territory) Act 1984 (Act 303), and others. Each state has enactments and practice directions similar to the Federal Territory Acts, if not more.

Fourth, ensure and maintain access to a set of reported court decisions. It is helpful to have access to Islamic scholars or former Syariah judges to assist with doctrinal aspects of the argument.

Finally, understand judicial review. This mechanism allows members of the public, who are dissatisfied with a public authority's decision or ruling, to challenge its legality in court. Since a Syariah court is a public authority and an inferior tribunal, they fall under the High Court's supervisory jurisdiction, making it a subject to judicial review. A Syariah court decision is open to judicial review if it is tainted by illegality, irrationality, or procedural impropriety.

There have been undoubted frustrations in the years since I have worked as a Syariah practitioner. But there have been moments of pleasure, particularly concerning the learning and advisory aspect. I also have no regrets since donning my Syariah robes to practice, for it has certainly made my work and life more interesting and varied. It has given me an added dimension as a lawyer, and opened up a new landscape of law and life to explore.

Long may it continue to be a part of my repertoire, Insyallah.

The Non-Practising Advocate and Solicitor

There are many categories of people in the practise of law.

One of those comprise law graduates who either, for one, have never bothered to be qualified as lawyers; two, have qualified but did not practise; or, three, left soon after tasting the potion of practise.

Those in in the first category often mistake, if not insist, that completing an undergraduate law course is a sufficient qualification for entering into the arcane practice of law. This is a mistake because they have no comprehension that the practice of law is a different, nastier, more aggressive beast than its comparatively genteel study. A similar comparison would be playing with a kitten and trying to kill a tiger with nothing except your shredded loincloth .

Any respectable practising lawyer will tell you that an undergraduate degree is a proof that you survived the course and paid enough attention to pass your exams during that three-year holiday that masqueraded as a degree. The sole function of it is to help you slide your foot into the narrow opening of the entrance door to the legal realm. It is important to understand that a degree does not enable you to pass.

To do so, you need to take a professional exam. In England, it is the Bar course (for barristers, a court-going lawyer) or a legal practice course (for solicitors, who generally do not go to court and handle corporate and conveyancing transactions). In Singapore, you have the Postgraduate Practical Law Course or PLC. In Malaysia, it is the dreaded roulette called the Certificate of Legal Practise, more popularly known among budding lawyers as the Legal Qualifying Exam of Death (because of the high failure rate), which really should be run by a casino instead of the Legal Profession Qualifying Board of Malaysia.

When you pass the relevant exams, only then can a lowly law graduate remotely identify themselves as a lawyer. A law graduate should not attempt to pass themselves off as one in the company of true lawyers, for they will come up short mighty quickly among them. If and when such posturing is discovered, the lawyers are entitled in equity, if not law, to laugh heartily and derogatorily at the law graduate's misplaced sense of occupation. They are also encouraged to point emphatically and ridicule the unfortunate law graduate for their benefit so this error is so seared into their minds that they never attempt such foolish a thing again.

After all, to be a lawyer is already bad enough; to pretend to be one is just criminal. It is heartening to know that impersonating a lawyer is an offence under section 205 of the Penal Code, punishable with a maximum of three years in prison and a fine, or both. So, if you hear a mere law graduate talk, walk, and spit like a lawyer, you are duty-bound to lodge a police report against them, more so if they can drink you under the table.

Referring those in category two as lawyers is as misguided as calling those who know how to fish but don't fish fishermen. If you stay home and play fishing games on your Wii machine, PlayStation, or Xbox, you are a gamer, not a fisherman.

Similarly, someone who is merely qualified to commence practice cannot be properly known as a lawyer because they have not yet practised the law. An accurate description for them would be 'someone qualified for the practice of law'. We should rightly refer to them as an SQPL, an ugly-looking, computer programming language-sounding abbreviation, that reflects their confusion of purpose about their intended career in law.

What then of those in category three? Surely, Encik Fahri, they are entirely deserving and entitled to refer to themselves as lawyers, and no doubt, some would fairly ask. After all, they are qualified and have some experience, never mind, how meagre or dull it may have been. Since they have tasted that practise of law, they now entirely deserve that right to think of and refer to themselves as lawyers, even though they may have devoted the rest of their career, if not life, to some other vocation, like politics, for example.

Even in this circumstance, you cannot. Can you seriously call yourself a fisherman if you only fished for a year and then spent the next thirty as a chief executive officer of a multinational company? Most often, people would describe you as a CEO, not a fisherman. To be known as a member of a profession necessitates devoting yourself to it. It is not enough to taste and know its flavour; it has to live in the belly. Before you can claim the title of any profession, you have to be in its guts. When you leave it, you can no longer claim the title.

Although, you can claim that you think, talk, and even swear like a lawyer, but you cannot claim to be one or represent yourself the same way. A lawyer is someone in legal practice: If that is not what you are doing, you are not a lawyer.

It is as simple as that.

Lately, I have noticed an unhealthy growing trend among those in categories two and three, who have moved on to other careers related to the legal profession (editors of legal journals, in-house legal executives, etc.) who state on their cards, in addition to their present vocation, 'non-practising advocate and solicitor'. I used to look upon it with bemusement, something that has now settled into amusement.

Why is it amusing?

Firstly, it suggests a desperate, futile attempt to associate oneself with an abandoned legal heritage—the practice of law. Using the words 'Advocate and Solicitor' serves as a reminder of what it could have been—even a scar of dreams dashed and intentions thwarted. It is amusing that these people choose to reveal a part of their inner selves so nakedly.

Secondly, to describe oneself as a 'non-practising advocate and solicitor' is not so much a description as it is a non-description. As a lawyer, I can put on my card 'non-practising shower scrubber', 'non-professional tennis player', 'non-charging credit card holder', or even 'non-sitting judge of the Federal Court' (since I'm qualified for the position but have not been appointed).

In short, you can put just about anything to describe yourself from the perspective of what you are not.

This is why the practice of stating your occupation, instead of what you are not occupied doing, came to develop. It is a sensible thing to do, but seems forgotten in this mad rush to burnish one's qualifications or credentials. I often note calling cards bearing such a non-description that include as many of their qualifications as possible, no matter how irrelevant. If they think that the three-day baking course they did at Aunty Kim's house the other day might improve others' impression of them from a professional or intellectual standpoint, you can bet your briefs (not the legal ones, of course) they will stick it in there.

So, why do they do it? I would like to know myself.

As a lawyer, my competency only extends to whether and why a person can describe themselves as an 'advocate and solicitor'. Why someone describes themselves as a 'non-practising advocate and solicitor' is not a legal issue, but rather a psychological one. A therapist is more appropriate to explain such issues, and by therapist, I naturally mean not a 'non-practising therapist'.

The Unbearable Heaviness of Being Right

At work, as a lawyer, I have to be right. If possible, all the time. If not, I should be right *most* of the time. At the very least, I have to be right more often than I am not. If not, I won't be a competent lawyer.

I have to be right in front of my staff in my office. If I am doing anything wrong, they will either not work for me or do so with resentment. If I had been wrong about managing the office, we wouldn't have been around as long as we have. Touchwood.

I also have to be right before my colleagues: the lawyers, the pupils, and the interns. If I am always wrong, I will not command their respect as a lawyer. They will not want to learn from me. There is only so much you can learn from the failures of others.

I have to be right about the advice I give my clients because a lawyer who is wrong is practically useless. You don't need to see a lawyer to get it wrong; you see a lawyer to get it right.

In a meeting room, negotiating a deal, I must be right about my client's interests and rights. On the other side, if they are not worth their salt, my colleague will insist on being right about their client's interests and rights. Being wrong on either side results in prejudice among our respective clients.

In court, when I stand up to argue, I have to be right—or at least righter than the other side. I have to be right about the facts and authorities I rely on and the arguments I advance, and the way I advance the argument, answer a query, or respond to an argument. If I don't, I am likely to lose, if I haven't already.

Ideally, as a lawyer, I should be right all the time. The rightness expected of me is as certain as night following day. Nobody wants a lawyer who gets it wrong all the time or most of the time, but someone who gets it right all the time. Lawyers who fit in the latter category are likelier to be lauded, feted, and admired. They are also likelier to have access to high-value disputes, interesting legal issues, and wealthier clients.

There is also a cost to getting it wrong, aside from being shunned. As a lawyer, I can be sued for negligence, that is, carelessness. If I *deliberately* do wrong, I leave myself vulnerable to a claim for fraud, cheating, or breach of trust.

So, lawyers do not just have to be right; they need to be right. At work, anyway.

I am not complaining about any of this. It's the nature of my profession—getting it right is part and parcel of being a lawyer. That's why lawyers (and by that, I mean proper ones) work hard at researching, understanding, formulating, drafting, advocacy, and the like. We also want to get it right, and in the right way, because that's all justice demands: for it be done and seem to be done.

But truth be told, it's not bad to have that expectation of being right and getting it right. There is an internal satisfaction in all of it: the confidence gained in ourselves, the fortification of our belief that we know something real about this world, and the sense of a firmer grasp of this reality we are confronted with. All these bring a deep-seated sense of confidence and authority to our existence.

But there is a danger to wanting to be right and being right all the time.

It lies in the burden of being right, of wanting to be right, of repeatedly proving to others and ourselves that we are right.

Firstly, there is a huge amount of stress and anxiety in getting it right for someone else. We are stressed from the efforts and expectations of being right and anxious about avoiding the wrong.

Recall a personal problem of ours. Imagine giving it to someone competent to deal with, knowing it will be taken care of, and you will not have to worry about it. That is the relief, peace of mind, and a degree of psychological comfort we are meant to provide by being right from a legal standpoint.

But that's our problem, and now, we are dealing with other people, while their reputations are at stake. Their company business owes or is owed money. Their constitutional rights were violated. They were sacked from their job. The stakes are usually high—it's not always just about money.

Although, we need to be right about that too.

So, we have a lot of responsibility. Done right, we shoulder their problem and relieve them of it for a while. Ultimately, it is their problem, unless, of course, we can come to terms on a reasonable lifetime retainer, then hello again, my old friend.

Secondly, there is a common lack of appreciation for the effort that goes into getting it right. A great deal of time, effort, thinking, and creativity goes into the same, not simply avoiding wrong—these are separate things. But avoiding wrong does not mean we got it right. So, it is not enough to avoid wrong, we need to get it right.

Getting it wrong is easy, but the other option always requires effort—a lot of effort. The problem for us lawyers when we get it right is that our work looks ridiculously obvious and easy, particularly for those not in the business of having to be right about the law. They are seduced into thinking they can save expenses by mimicking what they see.

'Of course, that's how it's done! It's so obvious! Just cut and paste!'

Tragically, they often belatedly discover that paying to get it right costs much more than not paying and getting it wrong. There's a reason why people with sick money have lawyers advise them. They know it's cheaper to pay a lawyer to get it right early, than to suffer the risk of a more expensive wrong later, like putting out a little flame before it becomes a forest fire.

Thirdly, and more gravely, if we are not careful, being right becomes a habit, then an addiction, if not a downright disease. Getting it right, being right, and in the right way is corrupted and conflated into a sense of perpetual self-righteousness.

We become intolerant of dissent or a different view, often getting angry whenever someone heightens our cognitive dissonance. We aggressively reject any intrusion of reality into our worldview. Instead, we annoy, mock, bully, and berate others into conceding that we are right. We are constantly wrestling with our cognitive dissonance.

It is no longer about getting it right, but insisting it. Each moment of engagement with someone is a fresh opportunity to reinforce that—from the trivial to the significant. We become insufferable. Our families can't stand us, and we have a handful of people we can call friends.

The Malays have an apt description for this pathology: *bodoh sombong* or stupid arrogant. Their arrogance leaves them stupid. What is stupid? In his book *The Basic Laws of Human Stupidity*, Carlo Cipolla, a professor of economic history, defined it thus:

> A stupid person is one who causes harm to another person or group without at the same time obtaining a benefit for himself or even damaging himself. [41]

Insisting we are right all the time leads to stupidity. A stupid lawyer is an ineffective lawyer, who is a waste of time and money.

Finally, there is the danger of forgetting that there are more things to life than being right. Being right is not the be-all and end-all; it's not the whole story. And cruelty is inherent to being right, especially when we know we are wrong.

Just because I got it right and you didn't does not suddenly entitle me to disrespect you, berate you, demean you, or think myself to be better than you. Those obsessed with being right forget that it does not relieve us of our obligation to be respectful, understanding, and humble about what we think we know. My being right in this instant doesn't mean I will now do so every moment henceforth. It may suggest I am likelier to get it right next time. That's it. Investment houses always caution: past performance is no guarantee of future performance.

Even those who are always right have to take a left occasionally. If they don't, they go in circles.

Being right once doesn't have a halo effect on our other qualities. It doesn't make us cleverer, more beautiful, fitter, or more intelligent. But it does tend to corrupt us—we become uglier, impatient, dismissive, and disrespectful. Observe those who always insist they are right: Are they nice? Far from a 'halo' effect, it tends to have an 'asshole' effect.

We may not have a choice about getting it right or being right at work but let us not forget that outside the confines of

---

[41] Carlo Cipolla (2019) 'Second Basic Law', in The Basic Laws of Human Stupidity. WH Allen.

work, in life, there is more to it than just being right. The path to being right is relatively narrow and straight compared to a plurality of paths to being wrong or getting it wrong. But there are other paths, too: The meandering ways of exploration, understanding, empathy, and compassion, which lead to vistas of an open mind, beauty, and ideas.

Only when we take the time and trouble to walk these other paths can we, for a moment, suspend the unbearable heaviness of being right and appreciate that in life, there is far more beauty in being appropriate than right. If we walk them enough, we appreciate that being right, getting it right, is simply a piece of a larger whole.

Just as we are.

The Crowning Glory of a Legal Career

When I started my legal practice in Malaysia, I thought being appointed a judge would be the crowning glory of my career. By judge, I do not mean Magistrates', Sessions, or Syariah courts judges; I mean a superior court judge, a High Court judge, a Court of Appeal judge, or a Federal Court judge.

Back then, I imagined patiently working my way through the litigation ranks, from pupil to lawyer, to able lawyer, to senior and experienced lawyer who is recognized for integrity, intelligence, industry, independence, and intrepidity. The judiciary would eventually recognize and acknowledge my qualities with an invitation to the bench.

I would write judgments that were read not just for their *ratio decidendi*[42], but for literary merit too, because mine would be witty, pithy, yet incisive—laced with profound insights into the Malaysian politico-legal milieu or compulsive legal thrillers. They would have you at the edge of your seat, contemplating how the decision would emerge until the very last line.

I would break new legal ground, not just in substance, but in form. I would pioneer the picture judgment, a judgment without words composed entirely of a deft, meaningful sequential arrangement of pictures. With my infamous controversial mime judgment, I would put Malaysia on the map,

[42] The rationale of the court's decision.

delivering my grounds of a decision using gesture, expression, and movement in a skintight black velvet bodysuit with a little skull motif on the inner lining of the cape.

My justice-infused phrases would smear the general national consciousness through memes, T-shirts, windshield stickers, lesser-known legal journals, and mugs with metal caps. My judgments would be vigorously discussed and settled through fistfights in coffee shops, outside massage parlours, and in private urinals nationwide.

Like the great English jurist, Lord Denning, I too would pontificate about the law in my books, despite my backlog of written grounds and colleagues looking at me askance. And maybe, a massive *maybe*, if the geo-political, domestic political, cultural, societal, legal, and royal factors coincidentally coalesced and collided into a miracle, I might even ascend from the far reaches of the Tawau High Court, my first posting and after occupying it for the majority of my career, to the very top.

I hope for a tenure of at least ninety-three days to avoid the dubious honour of being the shortest-serving chief justice.

The short and simple truth is that, back then, I thought being a judge was the thing. I considered judgeship to be the highest privilege and honour one could achieve in legal practice.

The traditional idea that a judge, having presided over the arena of conflict for many years, would not do well to be seen near the arena floor resonated with me. Mastery does not automatically follow from mere proximity and observation. Hearing swords clanging from a distance does not build endurance to swing away in a loincloth at close quarters. After rising to the top, one doesn't drop back into the bog. After beating about as a butterfly, the butterfly does not crawl like a caterpillar again. Have you ever seen that happen? I haven't. But I imagine it is awkward, bizarre, and disturbing.

But as with many things in Malaysia, that tradition has eroded, corroded, and been turned on its head. I now contend that the crowning glory of a legal career is not judgeship but being a lawyer. I also contend this state of affairs is the doing of our retired judges: It is becoming uncomfortably common for a retired judge to get called as an advocate and solicitor, and then plead in the very courts they presided over before. They fail to realize that by doing so, they reduce, lessen, and debase their former position's prestige, distinction, and exclusivity.

I want to highlight the traditional arguments against judges returning to court practice as a reminder of why it was prohibited in the first place because I feel it has been forgotten.

Firstly, judges are not encouraged or motivated to see through their full term. Judges who cannot go back to practice are likelier to see through their full term. Allowing such a thing encourages those who join the judiciary to retire early and use their former appointment to improve their employability or earning capacity as lawyers.

I am often advised about this when we somehow get on to whether I want to or should apply for a judgeship or judicial commissionership with well-meaning colleagues at the Bar.

'Fahri, you should go into the judiciary. After you complete your service as a judicial commissioner/judge, you can command greater fees because you have experience and contacts with the judiciary. You don't even have to be a Court of Appeal or Federal Court judge! You can command a higher fee even if you were previously a serving judicial commissioner or judge.'

That is not a reason to be a judge—improve future earnings as a counsel after retirement. With respect, I think that is a poor, if not disgusting, reason to join the judiciary. Those who do so have a damaging long-term impact on the judiciary. Such thinking would lead to a high judiciary turnover rate, taking judicial office for collateral reasons other than public service. This, in turn, brings a lack of stability and predictability about judicial affairs, policy, and trends, leaving it politically vulnerable, which is dangerous in a Malaysian setting.

This setting provides opportunities for judges to curry favour with litigants or lawyers in the years leading up to their retirement as part of their career planning. This distracts them from concentrating on their work and maintaining their integrity. If judges decide with one eye on their exit, they are likely to favour certain legal positions or litigants over others, and it will inhibit, if not skew, their decision-making.

For example, if, as a judge, I keep ruling for a rich and powerful corrupt politician, I can better make a case that he should hire me as his lawyer after I retire from the bench or that would be my reward after retirement.

It is not whether the judge does it but whether they are allowed the opportunities to do so.

Secondly, it is unfair to go up against former judges, especially former office holders, such as a retired chief judge of Sabah and Sarawak, chief judge of Malaya, president of the Court of Appeal, or chief justice.

Consider this: You pit an unknown lawyer who has been practising for five years against a former Chief Justice. In a 50/50, who do you think the judge hearing the matter is likelier to decide for? Who is he more likely to give the benefit of the doubt to—an unknown lawyer or a former chief justice?

The opportunity and ease of choosing the latter over the former is available. Even if I am overruled on appeal, I can say, 'Hey, I relied on the former chief justice's argument.'

Optics-wise, it looks far better to be wrong about a former chief justice's argument than that of a nobody. Which is easier to go with? This, thus, creates a strong temptation for bias.

I am inclined to think that allowing former judges and former office bearer judges back into active litigation breaches the equality provision in Article 8(1) of the Federal Constitution, which provides that all persons are equal before the law and entitled to equal protection of the law.

It breaches this provision because achieving such equality in court is impossible when it involves a former office-bearing judge. Any lawyer who has never been a judge will never be equal from an institutional perspective, compared to someone who formerly held a high office. It will always be asymmetrical, because the former judge benefits from their previous judicial experience, prestige, and instinctual, if not institutional, connections which the lawyer lacks. This creates an unequal playing field. The fair treatment of the counsels does not neutralize the judicial deference the former judge is likely to have compared to an unknown lawyer.

Thirdly, there is the embarrassment of a former judge having to argue against their decisions or take legal positions against their previous rulings. This inevitably calls into question the lawyer's competency or credibility as a judge then, and his ethics as a lawyer now.

Fourthly, there is the issue of the public interest. How would an ordinary public member perceive a former judge arguing against a lawyer? I am confident most would bet on the former judge to win. Right or wrong, this is the perceived effect of their involvement. If they believe this—and based on my anecdotal experience, they will—justice is no longer seen to be served. It doesn't matter whether it actually is; as far as the public is concerned, it hasn't been. It becomes an unfair battle. A *Tun* versus *Tuan* situation.[43]

[43] In Malaysia, *Tun* is the highest honour that can be given. In Malay, *Tuan* is the equivalent of 'Mister'.

This perception does not accrue favourably to the judiciary as a whole, for it damns the doctrine of judicial impartiality. A judge must continue upholding the dignity of the judicial profession even during retirement because their personality is closely associated with it. They remain a symbol of the judiciary even after they have left.

Ultimately, this matter should be decided with the public interest in mind, not the former judge's private interest prioritized. I remain steadfastly of the view that former judges, of whatever rank, should not appear in courts. When we make such assessments, we must not take the best example of a judge or lawyer but bear in mind the worst of them, too. This is a realistic notion.

And why should former judges persist with court work, anyway? It is not as though they cannot do anything else. There is enough non-court private dispute resolution work for them, such as arbitration and mediation. There is also enough advisory, speaking, teaching, and consulting work. In other words, much other work can be done instead of court work.

Judges receive a pension after they retire. If they were in government or legal service before their elevation, they can still avail it. If they were high-flying lawyers before, they would have savings from their previous legal practice, which would be enough compensation for them to stay away from court work. The inability to do anything else demonstrates a lack of imagination, a small and rigid circle of competency, or an inherent insufficient respect for their previous office.

My view is not the prevailing one. But it is shared by the Malaysian Bar in its resolution passed on 15 March 2014, in a motion proposed by V.C. George and Razlan Hadri Zulkifli, which reads:

> (1) That a retired judge of the superior courts should be prohibited or restricted by law from appearing as counsel in court, and to achieve that objective calls on the incoming Bar Council to propose an amendment of the Legal Profession Act 1976 to the Attorney General for urgent presentation to Parliament . . .

The seemingly prevailing legal position in Malaysia is that there is no Bar for a former judge to return to practice as a lawyer, no matter how high the office. This was decided by the Federal Court in 2013 when the Bar Council objected to Dato' Sri Gopal Sri Ram acting for Dato' Anwar Ibrahim in his sodomy appeal before the Federal Court.

The good thing about that decision was there were no written grounds. That means, as a source of precedent, that decision is worthless in light of the Federal Court decision of *Tetuan Wan Shahrizal, Hari & Co. v PP* [2023] 4 CLJ 843, which held:

> Thus, where there are no grounds written, there is no point or principle of law that can officially be decided or settled by the ruling of a competent court. The correct position of the law is that an unwritten decision of a higher court, whether sitting in its original or appellate jurisdiction, binds the parties to the action but is not authority for any principle or rule of law and does not bind the lower courts.

That means this issue is still open for consideration, submission, and an authoritatively written decision by the courts. There is effectively no binding decision about it.

This new normal of former judges returning to practice was marked by the former Chief Justice, Tun Md Raus Sharif's call to the Bar on 17 January 2023 at the age of 72. He was robed by Tan Sri Zulkefli Ahmad Makinudin, who served as the president of the Court of Appeal during his tenure as chief justice. Tan Sri Zulkefli was also called to the Bar after his retirement on 12 March 2021 and has appeared in the courts as counsel.

These two were the top judicial officers who, having reached such heights, were now back in court as lawyers. Tun Md Raus Sharif's call to the Bar was significant because it was the first admission of a top former judge as a lawyer since Tun Salleh Abbas, after the latter was unceremoniously removed from office in 1988.

Interestingly, the former speakers of Parliament, Tan Mohamad Ariff bin Md Yusof (16 July 2018 to 13 July 2020) and Tan Sri Azhar Azizan Harun (13 July 2020 to 18 December 2022), returned to legal practice after completing their tenure, with the latter making court appearances.

Thankfully, we do not have any former prime ministers who want to be admitted as lawyers after their tenures. However, Malaysia's first three prime ministers were legally trained and called to the English Bar. Tunku Abdul Rahman and Tun Abdul Razak went straight into government legal service after their return. Only Tun Hussein Onn appears to have had a stint of legal practice before becoming the prime minister.

From history and the behaviour of more recent former judges and Parliamentary speakers, we can appreciate how the prestige of the legal profession has reached such lofty heights: Those who served at the highest levels of parliament and the judiciary (two out of three of the organs of government) want to be lawyers. Although the legal profession does not yet have the dubious distinction of having a former prime minister wanting to be admitted as a lawyer, the legal profession is the place for them to spring forth from.

Nowadays, if you ask me what is the crowning glory of a legal career in Malaysia, my answer would be simple.

It's being an advocate and solicitor, a lawyer.

Retired chief justices, presidents of the Court of Appeal, Federal Court judges, Court of Appeal judges, High Court judges, and even the transitory judicial commissioner want to appear in court as counsel. Speakers of Parliament want to be lawyers again. Prime ministers of Malaysia were lawyers.

It's mad. But it's Malaysia.

This situation is the best thing for people like me who are unlikely to make it to the bench or reach high office and won't amount to much in life. I don't have to go through a career at the bench, serve time in Parliament or any government ministry to get to where they are.

I am already there.

I've been here all along.

Acknowledgements

I thank my editor, Amberdawn Manaois, for her thoughtful suggestions; Nora Nazerene and Penguin South East Asia for publishing my work. It is a dream come true, and it still feels surreal.

I thank all of you who read me for your support, encouragement, comments, corrections, and recommendations. You keep me motivated to keep at it. I especially acknowledge and thank Cheow Wee for regularly reading and pointing out my grammatical errors.

I thank my parents for encouraging me to read and buying all the books I asked for.

I thank my wife, Lee Siew May, for her support, patience, and sustenance. Were it not for her able management of my family life, keeping the kids at bay, ensuring I'm well-fed and hassling me to sleep early, I would not have the time, energy, and space to think, write, and edit. Thank you, baby.